THE URBANA

D0061419

On the Road: Surviving the Loss of a Spouse

Sheryl Garrett, CFP®
Series Editor

Adapted and compiled
Ruth J. Mills

Dearborn
Trade Publishing
A **Kaplan Professional** Company

3-06
$16.00

President, Dearborn Publishing: Roy Lipner
Vice President and Publisher: Cynthia A. Zigmund
Senior Acquisitions Editor: Mary B. Good
Cover Design: Design Solutions

© 2006 by Dearborn Financial Publishing, Inc.

Published by Dearborn Trade Publishing
A Kaplan Professional Company

A Stonesong Press Book

Project Manager: Ellen Schneid Coleman
Interior Design: Brad Walrod/High Text Graphics, Inc.

Printed in the United States of America

06 07 08   10 9 8 7 6 5 4 3 2 1

Library of Congress Cataloging-in-Publication Data
Surviving the loss of a spouse/edited by Sheryl Garrett; adapted and compiled by Ruth J. Mills.
    p.   cm.—(On the road)
    Includes index.
    ISBN 1-4195-0042-2 (5 × 7.375 pbk.)
    1. Widows—Finance, Personal.   2. Widowers—Finance, Personal.
I. Garrett, Sheryl.   II. Mills, Ruth J.   III. On the road (Chicago, Ill.)
HG179.S866 2006
332.024'0086'54—dc22   2005022392

Contents

Introduction

On the Road: Surviving the Loss of a Spouse is part of a new series of books from Dearborn Trade Publishing intended to help you deal with the financial issues, problems, and decisions concerning specific life events. The financial decisions you face after the death of your husband or wife are obviously different from the decisions you made earlier in your life to send your child to college or to buy a home, for example. Still, financial planning shouldn't be intimidating—especially at this difficult time of your life.

On the Road books are like travel guides to help you make the best financial decisions at each stage of your life—in this case, for how to get on with the rest of your life and make sure you and your children or other family members are protected financially. The emotional grief you're suffering is very painful, but this book can help you make the necessary financial decisions rationally, so that you can deal with insurance issues, retirement funds, and investing your remaining assets to make sure you have the money you need for the next phase of your life.

This book addresses the financial issues that concern you *now, including how to*:

1. organize your finances so that you can pay your bills, set up a new recordkeeping system, and establish a relationship with your financial service providers;
2. develop a meaningful budget, to help you adjust to the loss of your spouse's income and to replace the household services that spouse provided (childcare, laundry, yard work, and household repairs, for example);
3. update your long-term financial plan, to ensure that you and your loved ones are doing the right things now to prepare for your future;
4. protect your assets, by updating all your insurance: life, health, disability, homeowners', and automobile insurance; and
5. reassess your savings and investments, to ensure you have the right mix of stocks, bonds, mutual funds, real estate, or specialty investments.

By now you have probably begun the probate process with your attorney, or may have even already settled the estate. There are several good resources listed in Appendix B that can help you get through the probate process, and of course your attorney is available to help you as well. This book addresses the issues that concern you now.

These financial decisions are part of your life's journey. We've made them easy to navigate with lots of helpful "Roadmaps" (charts and tables of financial information to help you with each issue or decision that comes up) and "Tollbooths" that help you calculate your expenses or savings, as well as "Hazard" signs that caution you on money pitfalls to watch out for. We've included "What to Pack" so that you'll know what forms or other information you need, for example, to update your will. There are "Postcards" that tell helpful and inspiring stories of how other widows and widowers have made this particularly difficult financial journey successfully. We've made sure you'll know what we're talking about by providing "Learn the Language" definitions of unfamiliar or technical terms particular to each financial topic.

Finally, we've included an "Itinerary," a recap of all the key actions you should take—all of which are covered in detail in the five chapters of this book. At the end we have included a list of other books and resources you can turn to if you want more in-depth information on such topics as finding qualified financial planners or estate planning lawyers. We hope you find this "travel" guide helpful as you map your route to financial success and peace of mind during and after this difficult time. So let's get started on making sure you get what you need for this part of your life's journey.

Moving on Down the Road

Organize Your Finances

The emotional trauma of losing a spouse can be life shattering. But the financial consequences might be even more devastating. In many (if not most) marriages, one person typically handles the "family finances"—which means the other person may be ill-informed or ill-prepared to handle the many complex aspects of personal finance when their spouse dies.

If you are in such a situation, you must work quickly to reassemble your financial foundation. So much needs to be done when you are least able to cope. You must collect on life insurance policies; work with estate lawyers, trustees, and probate courts; assess your investment portfolio and possibly establish your own credit identity among other things. These overwhelming circumstances can make you particularly vulnerable to misleading or self-serving advice from financial product salespeople presenting themselves as objective financial advisors. By walking you through what you need to do first, you'll become more informed and this chapter can help you get organized about your immediate financial responsibilities and fulfill your current obligations.

▶ Map Your Route

Whenever you undergo a major change in your family situation, particularly the death of your spouse, it is important to take stock of where you stand financially. As a widow or widower, you will inherit some or all of your spouse's assets, depending on the estate planning you and your spouse may have done. This may dramatically change your net worth, as well as your cash flow and budgets. If you receive a life insurance settlement, your assets will rise by the amount of the death benefit. However, if your spouse received payments from a life annuity without a term certain payout option, annuity payments will cease. Therefore, it's important to redo your net worth, cash flow, and budgeting statements to account for your changed circumstances. We'll walk you through that in Chapter 2, but just keep it in mind for now.

Stop #1: Locate Important Papers and Set Up a Recordkeeping System

Getting a handle on your financial situation will be much easier if you don't have to dig through boxes full of unopened bank and brokerage statements, life insurance records, and old tax returns. Although it will take some effort at first to stay organized during this difficult emotional time (when you quite possibly don't feel like doing anything at all), the time commitment will be minimal compared to the return you will earn from getting a handle on your finances. It is also invaluable to have your papers easily accessible for probate purposes or when you are filling out your tax return. Plus, staying organized can be a useful distraction from your grief; many people find that getting organized at this time is immensely helpful in their grieving process. In fact, some feel they would become even more depressed if their financial papers became overwhelming.

A recordkeeping worksheet is particularly useful because it consolidates all your important information in one place, including lists of telephone numbers and addresses of all the professional advisors and family members you should contact immediately. If you don't have such a worksheet, you should create one now. Roadmap 1.1 provides a sample; you can simply fill in the blanks.

If you don't already have a filing system, you should establish one. What you need is a filing system separate from the rest of your household files with an individual file for each category described in the Recordkeeping Work-

Dear Naomi,

Since Peter died, I just haven't been able to face the mountain of bills and other financial papers. I know I need to, but they're just overwhelming. And I realize I should have gotten more involved in our banking and investments, but because I handled so many of the other household responsibilities, I was just grateful that Peter took care of paying the bills.

Now that he's gone, I'm half worried that if I don't find the bill and pay it soon the electric company will simply shut off my lights one of these days. I also have to take care of Peter's life insurance policy, and have to call his company's HR department to find out about his retirement benefits. And frankly, I don't even think I can pick up the phone. Do you think you could help me get organized? I'd really appreciate it, so please let me know.

Thanks,
Ruth

sheet in Roadmap 1.1. It is crucial to note on the worksheet where all your important documents are located and other details such as account numbers and the names of your financial planner, brokers, insurance agents, and other people who know about your accounts. Even worse, if something happens to you soon after the death of your spouse, it will be extremely difficult for your children or other beneficiaries to assemble your financial records.

Stop #2: Organize and Pay Your Bills

Many people in the first stages of grieving find it difficult to handle routine activities on a regular basis—yet the world in which we live demands that we do things like pay our bills on time. To make this task easier, you might consider setting up an online bill-paying system or establishing a program through your bank so that your bills will be paid automatically. This will be one less thing you'll have to worry about. (Appendix B offers a list of such services, with contact and other information.)

There are a variety of ways to utilize online bill payment, but overall it boils down to three general options:

1. *Your current bank.* With most banks, you can pay each bill as a onetime bill, set up payments for recurring bills, pay multiple bills at one time, and even set up future periodic payments. If you are using a personal finance software program for managing your budget, there generally is a whole section devoted to helping you connect with your bank. With this bank connection, you will be able to regularly download the information from your bank to the software on your computer, so that you can update your current financial records. Most major banks offer online banking services.

2. *The companies themselves.* You can go directly to your credit card or utility company's Web site to sign up for their bill payment services. Essentially, you are giving permission to both the company and your bank to exchange the necessary financial information. When you give the go-ahead the company will electronically go to your bank and get the payment from your account.

3. *Aggregation services.* These companies (Quicken and Mvelopes are two examples) offer their own independent online services, including bill payment, directly to customers. Their service will gather (i.e., "aggregate") and link all the various Web sites where you have online account information, such as your bank, credit card companies, utilities, mortgage company, investments, and 401(k) account, and make them all conveniently available on one secure Web site. Using the bill payment feature along with an aggregation service makes it convenient for you to pay all your bills from one Web site and have access to all your other financial records.

▶ Take on Passengers

If you find you need a little extra help getting your bills, finances, and records in order, don't fret—you are not the only one. Most people feel this way. If you are looking for that extra help, make sure you hire the *right* person—someone you can trust—to help you with what you really need. Right now, finding a lawyer to sort through any potential probate issues is your #1 priority. Once you've done that you can focus on the specific financial issues that you need to address.

Recordkeeping Worksheet

1. Personal Information

Your Name _____
Spouse's Name _____
Address _____
Home Telephone _____
Work Telephone/FAX _____
Date, Place of Birth _____
Birth Certificate Location _____
Social Security Number _____
Marital Status _____

Your Father's Name _____
Spouse's Name _____
Address _____
Home Telephone _____
Work Telephone/FAX _____
Date, Place of Birth _____
Birth Certificate Location _____
Social Security Number _____
Marital Status _____

Your Mother's Name _____
Spouse's Name _____
Address _____
Home Telephone _____
Work Telephone/FAX _____
Date, Place of Birth _____
Birth Certificate Location _____
Social Security Number _____
Marital Status _____

Your Sibling's Name(s) _____
Spouse's Name _____
Address _____
Home Telephone _____
Work Telephone/FAX _____
Date, Place of Birth _____
Birth Certificate Location _____
Social Security Number _____
Marital Status _____

Recordkeeping Worksheet

Your Child's Name(s) _____
Spouse's Name _____
Address _____
Home Telephone _____
Work Telephone/FAX _____
Date, Place of Birth _____
Birth Certificate Location _____
Social Security Number _____
Marital Status _____

Sibling's Child's Name(s) _____
Spouse's Name _____
Address _____
Home Telephone _____
Work Telephone/FAX _____
Date, Place of Birth _____
Birth Certificate Location _____
Social Security Number _____
Marital Status _____

2. Professional Contacts
Accountant _____
Address _____
Telephone/FAX _____
Assistant's Name _____

Attorney _____
Address _____
Telephone/FAX _____
Assistant's Name _____

Banker _____
Address _____
Telephone/FAX _____
Assistant's Name _____

Dentist _____
Address _____
Telephone/FAX _____
Assistant's Name _____

Employee Benefits Counselor
Address _____
Telephone/FAX _____
Assistant's Name _____

Executor of Estate
Address _____
Telephone/FAX _____
Assistant's Name _____

Financial Planner
Address _____
Telephone/FAX _____
Assistant's Name _____

Insurance Agent (auto)
Address _____
Telephone/FAX _____
Assistant's Name _____

Insurance Agent (health)
Address _____
Telephone/FAX _____
Assistant's Name _____

Insurance Agent (home)
Address _____
Telephone/FAX _____
Assistant's Name _____

Insurance Agent (life)
Address _____
Telephone/FAX _____
Assistant's Name _____

Investment Manager
Address _____
Telephone/FAX _____
Assistant's Name _____

Physician
Address _____
Telephone/FAX _____
Assistant's Name _____

Priest/Rabbi/Minister
Address _____
Telephone/FAX _____
Assistant's Name _____

Recordkeeping Worksheet

Stockbroker _____
Address _____
Telephone/FAX _____
Assistant's Name _____

Trust Officer _____
Address _____
Telephone/FAX _____
Assistant's Name _____

Other _____
Address _____
Telephone/FAX _____
Assistant's Name _____

Other _____
Address _____
Telephone/FAX _____
Assistant's Name _____

3. Financial Accounts

Banking Records (CDs, checking, credit union, savings)

Name of Institution	Type of Account	Account Number	Location of Documents
_____	_____	_____	_____
_____	_____	_____	_____
_____	_____	_____	_____
_____	_____	_____	_____

Bonds (corporate, municipal, Treasury bonds)

Issuer	# of Bonds	Due Date	Location of Documents
_____	_____	_____	_____
_____	_____	_____	_____
_____	_____	_____	_____

Business Ownership

Name of Business	Type of Business	% Owned	Other Partners	Location of Documents
_____	_____	_____	_____	_____
_____	_____	_____	_____	_____

Children's Accounts

Child's Name	Trustee	Type of Account or Trust	Location of Funds

Debts (auto, credit card, education, mortgage)

Type of Loan	Name of Institution	Account Number	Amount Due	Monthly Payment

Employee Benefit and Retirement Plans (401(k), IRA, Keogh plans, pension plans, profit-sharing plans, stock purchase plans)

Type of Plan	Who Is Covered	Trustee	$ Value of Plan	Beneficiary(ies)

Insurance Policies (auto, health, home, life insurance)

Type of Policy	Insures Who or What	Name of Company	Account Number	Location of Documents

Mutual Funds

Type of Account	Name of Company	Account Number	Location of Documents

Real Estate

Type of Property	Location of Property	Date Purchased	Purchase Price $ Plus Cost of Improvements	Location of Documents

Roadmap 1.1 (continued)

Recordkeeping Worksheet

Safe-Deposit Boxes

Depository Bank and Address	Primary and Secondary Owner of Assets	Person with Power of Attorney	Location of Contents List and Key
_____	_____	_____	_____
_____	_____		_____
_____	_____	_____	_____
_____	_____		

Stocks

Type of Account	Name of Company	Account Number	Location of Documents
_____	_____	_____	_____
_____	_____	_____	_____
_____	_____	_____	_____
_____	_____	_____	_____
_____	_____	_____	_____
_____	_____	_____	_____

Tax Records

Persons Filing	Estimated Quarterly Payments	Location of Latest Tax Return and Records	Location of Previous Returns
_____	_____	_____	_____
_____	_____	_____	_____
_____	_____	_____	_____
_____	_____	_____	_____

Wills and Trust Documents (LPOAs, health and financial, living wills, funeral directives)

Family Member Covered	Attorney	Executor	Location of Documents
_____	_____	_____	_____
_____	_____	_____	_____
_____	_____	_____	_____
_____	_____	_____	_____
_____	_____	_____	_____

4. Other Important Papers

Location

Address _____

Appliance Instructions,
Guarantees, and
Warranties _____

Automobile Titles or
Lease Documents _____

Burial Plot Documentation _____

Citizenship Papers/
Passports _____

Club Membership
Records _____

Contracts _____

Credit Reports _____

Divorce Decrees _____

Educational Records and
Diplomas _____

Employment Records _____

Financial Records _____

Frequent Flier Account
Records _____

Health Care Proxy _____

Health Records _____

Home Improvement
Records _____

Inventories of Household
Goods _____

Jury Duty Records _____

Living Wills _____

Marriage Certificate _____

Medical Insurance Forms _____

Medicare Cards _____

Military Discharge Papers _____

Power of Attorney
Documents _____

Receipts for Major
Purchases _____

Religious Information _____

Rental Leases _____

Résumés _____

Social Security Cards and
Earnings Records _____

Utility Bills _____

Other (specify) _____

At this point, financially speaking, you probably need only someone with bookkeeping experience or possibly an accountant, so let's look at that first. In later chapters, we'll cover additional advisors you'll need—especially a lawyer to help you with any immediate needs you may have arising from the death of your spouse and eventually with your will and estate planning —and probably a financial advisor. But right now, you simply need to take care of your immediate financial situation.

Stop #3: Find an Accountant

When your spouse dies, you probably will have to file several tax returns: a *federal estate tax return,* a *state inheritance tax return* in states that impose inheritance taxes, and your *personal federal* and *state income tax returns.* You must file an estate tax return if your spouse leaves an estate worth more than $2 million in 2006 (rising to $3.5 million in 2009). Working with an accountant and filing all these returns are probably the chores you least want to undertake after losing your spouse, but it must be done if you want to avoid penalties. The returns must be filed according to federal and state rules.

Therefore, you may want to hire an accountant to help you with your tax returns. Several rules in the tax code are specially designed for widows and widowers. For tax purposes, a widow or widower is considered unmarried and therefore usually must file the return as a single person. If you lost your spouse in the last two years, however, you may submit a return using the married filing-jointly status (usually more advantageous than single status) if you meet the following four conditions:

1. If you continue to maintain a primary home for a dependent child, and you provide at least half of the living costs of that child;
2. If you are entitled to claim that child as a dependent;
3. If you could have filed a joint return in the year your spouse died; and
4. If you have not remarried by January 1 of the following tax year. For example, in filing your 2006 tax return, you can use married status if you do not remarry before January 1, 2007.

As the surviving spouse of a married couple that filed jointly, you inherit all the income tax liabilities of your marriage. If you find it to your advantage, file as head of household once you are on your own. To do so, you must support at least half of a dependent child's living expenses. Your spouse must have died in a year prior to the current tax year and you must have filed jointly in the year your spouse died. Widows or widowers younger than age 65 who support children on an annual income of $12,800 or less need not file a tax return. Widows or widowers age 65 and older who support children need not file a return if their annual income is $13,750 or less.

Stop #4: Contact All Relevant Financial Personnel and Institutions

Finally, you need to notify various financial organizations that your spouse has passed away, so that they can update their own records. At the very least, you'll need to inform the following institutions:

▶ your spouse's employer, so that they can make arrangements regarding pension or other retirement plans as well as any outstanding salary or bonuses that may have been due to your spouse;

▶ your bank;

▶ your mortgage holder if you held a mortgage jointly with your spouse;

▶ your spouse's credit card companies and any companies in which you jointly had credit, so that those cards can be transferred solely to your name;

▶ your spouse's life insurance and medical insurance companies, Medicare, property, and automobile insurers (we'll cover insurance in more detail in Chapter 4);

▶ the Social Security Administration and Veterans Administration, if applicable;

▶ your spouse's attorney, financial planner, stockbroker and/or other investment advisors who might have been consulted. (We'll discuss working with your own financial planner in more detail in Chapters 3 and 5.)

If you feel that making these calls (or writing letters) may be emotionally difficult for you, that's perfectly understandable. The best option is to ask a family member or close friend to help you with this task.

▶ Looking Ahead

Now that you've gotten a handle on your immediate financial situation —you're organized with a recordkeeping system, you've paid your bills or made arrangements for them to be paid online and automatically, and you're aware of your tax situation—it's time to start thinking about the bigger picture: what you really have in terms of assets, what you owe in debts, and what your expenses are. In other words, it's time to look at your total net worth and create a budget for going forward.

Watch Out for Tolls

Develop a Meaningful Budget

This chapter takes a look at the bigger picture of your financial situation: where you are right now—what you have and what you owe; where you're headed—future expenses; and where you want to go—long-term investing goals. Don't be overwhelmed; we'll take this road slowly.

▶ Before You Go Anywhere, Where Are You Now?

Before you can make any decisions about your finances in the future, you should have a good idea of where you stand right now. In financial terms, that means calculating your net worth, and it's easier than it sounds. All you need to do is add up the total value of what you already own, which are your *assets,* and subtract the amount of debt you owe, which are your *liabilities.* This bottom line is known as your *net worth.* It is a snapshot in time, good only for the moment you calculate it. But that's all you need to concern yourself with right now: this moment in time.

By doing this calculation, you will be able to see clearly how your assets and liabilities match (or mismatch). If you find ways to reduce your spending, pay off your debts, and increase your savings and investment assets, you can make your net worth grow. If you are doing all the wrong things, like increasing your debt and depleting your savings, this will show up quickly in your net worth as well.

Calculating your net worth is also important because it lets you see at a glance whether you are accumulating enough assets to support yourself comfortably in the future. Having a current net worth statement will also come in handy when you apply for loans, such as a mortgage, or for financial aid for your children's college education, because lenders will require you to show your assets and liabilities on the application.

The High Road: Tallying Up Your Assets

There are five classes of assets. What distinguishes one kind from another is how quickly you can turn each into cash or, put another way, how liquid it is. The more liquid an asset, the easier it is to put a value on it. For instance, you know exactly what the $102.55 in your checking account is worth, but you will probably have to ask a local real estate agent or appraiser to give you the current worth of your house or apartment.

Roadmap 2.1 offers an Assets Worksheet to help you make a detailed list of not only your assets but also who holds the titles to them. Some assets, like a securities portfolio for a child, may be held in a trust for which a parent is responsible until the child turns 18. If you need more space for any category as you fill out the Roadmap, copy that page and attach it to your worksheet.

Because of the different levels of liquidity of different assets, we suggest you separate your assets into these five classes:

Current assets. Current assets are easily convertible into cash. This includes bank accounts, money-market mutual funds, and Treasury securities. For each of your own and your spouse's bank accounts, list the name of the bank where the asset is held, the balance, and the current yield. Also list the yield on Treasury bills, which mature in a year or less, and U.S. savings bonds, which you can cash in any time as long as you have held them for at least six months. If you have overpaid your taxes and are due a refund from the IRS or your state tax department, you should also count that as a current asset. If you are owed a bonus or commission within the next few months, that counts as current, too.

Securities. These include publicly traded stocks, bonds, mutual funds, futures contracts, warrants, and options. The current market values of all such securities are available in most major newspapers, particularly *The Wall Street Journal*, as well as from your broker or from stock quotation services such as

Roadmap 2.1

Assets Worksheet

Date _____

Assets	Date Purchased	Original $ Value/Cost	Current $ Value
1. Current Assets			
Bonuses or Commissions			
(due you)	_____	$_____	$_____
Certificates of Deposit	_____	_____	_____
	_____	_____	_____
Checking Accounts	_____	_____	_____
	_____	_____	_____
Credit Union Accounts	_____	_____	_____
Money-Market Accounts	_____	_____	_____
	_____	_____	_____
Savings Accounts	_____	_____	_____
	_____	_____	_____
Savings Bonds	_____	_____	_____
	_____	_____	_____
Tax Refunds (due you)	_____	_____	_____
Treasury Bills	_____	_____	_____
	_____	_____	_____
Total Current Assets		$_____	$_____
2. Securities			
Bonds (type of bond)			
_____	_____	$_____	$_____
_____	_____	_____	_____
_____	_____	_____	_____
_____	_____	_____	_____
Bond Mutual Funds			
_____	_____	_____	_____
Individual Stocks	_____	_____	_____
_____	_____	_____	_____
_____	_____	_____	_____
_____	_____	_____	_____
_____	_____	_____	_____
_____	_____	_____	_____
Stock Mutual Funds	_____	_____	_____
_____	_____	_____	_____
_____	_____	_____	_____
_____	_____	_____	_____
Futures	_____	_____	_____
Warrants and Options	_____	_____	_____
Total Securities		$_____	$_____

Assets	Date Purchased	Original $ Value/Cost	Current $ Value
3. Real Estate			
Mortgage Receivable			
(due you)	_____	$_____	$_____
Primary Residence	_____	_____	_____
Rental Property	_____	_____	_____
Real Estate Limited			
Partnerships	_____	_____	_____
Second Home	_____	_____	_____
Total Real Estate		$_____	$_____
4. Long-Term Assets			
Annuities	_____	$_____	$_____
IRAs	_____	_____	_____
Keogh Accounts	_____	_____	_____
Life Insurance Cash			
Values	_____	_____	_____
Loans Receivable			
(due you)	_____	_____	_____
Pensions	_____	_____	_____
Private Business			
Interests	_____	_____	_____
Profit-Sharing Plans	_____	_____	_____
Royalties	_____	_____	_____
Salary Reduction Plans			
(401(k), 403(b), 457			
plans)	_____	_____	_____
Total Long-term Assets		$_____	$_____
5. Personal Property			
Antiques	_____	$_____	$_____
Appliances (washing			
machines, dishwashers,			
vacuum cleaners, etc.)	_____	_____	_____
Automobiles	_____	_____	_____
Boats, etc.	_____	_____	_____
Campers, Trailers, etc.	_____	_____	_____
Clothing	_____	_____	_____
Coin Collections	_____	_____	_____
Computers, etc.	_____	_____	_____
Furniture	_____	_____	_____
Furs	_____	_____	_____
Home Entertainment			
Equipment (CD players,			
stereos, televisions,			
VCRs, etc.)	_____	_____	_____
Home Furnishings			
(drapes, blankets, etc.)	_____	_____	_____

Jewelry	_____	_____	_____
Lighting Fixtures	_____	_____	_____
Motorcycles, etc.	_____	_____	_____
Paintings and Sculptures	_____	_____	_____
Pools, etc.	_____	_____	_____
Stamp Collections	_____	_____	_____
Tableware (glasses, plates, silverware, etc.)	_____	_____	_____
Tools, etc.	_____	_____	_____
Other	_____	_____	_____
Total Personal Property		$ _____	$ _____
Total Assets		$ _____	$ _____

http://www.finance.yahoo.com. For each security, list your purchase price, the number of units (such as shares of stock) held, the percentage yield (a dividend for a stock, interest for a bond) it pays, when it matures (for a bond, a futures contract, or an option), and the balance.

Real estate. Real estate includes your primary and secondary (i.e., vacation) homes, condominiums, cooperatives, rental properties, real estate limited partnerships, and land. The current worth of all real estate should be based on appraisals from knowledgeable local experts like appraisers or estimates from real estate agents. Remember to subtract all selling costs, such as the standard 6 percent real estate broker's commission.

If you are a partner in any real estate ventures, list the general managing partner who is running the operation, the yield being paid to you, if any, and the year you expect the partnership to be liquidated and the proceeds paid out to you. Also include any mortgage loans that may be due you, such as on a house you sold on which you granted a loan.

Long-term assets. These include the cash value of life insurance policies; the worth of annuities, pensions, and profit-sharing plans; 401(k)s, IRAs and Keogh plans; any long-term loans due you; any long-term royalties due you from writing a book or patenting an invention that is still selling; and any interests you have in an ongoing business. Long-term assets are often difficult to value because you may not have access to them in several years, or even decades, from now.

Still, your life insurance company will give you the current cash value of policies and annuities, and your employer will tell you what your pension and profit-sharing plans would be worth if you left the company now. Valuing your interest in a closely held business is particularly tricky, but it can be done. Ask your partners what they would be willing to pay if you wanted to cash in your share. (To some extent, that depends on how actively involved in the business you are and how key it is for the business to have your services available.) You can also get some idea from a business broker who specializes in selling and buying the kind of business in which you are involved (but this is probably a little extreme for our purposes).

Personal property. Personal property such as cars, jewelry, collectibles, and home furnishings would be valued at whatever you think they could be sold for now in their present condition. In valuing personal property, try to be as realistic as possible. Don't just put down what you think they are worth; this number is often inflated. You should try to get some sense of the market when you value things. For instance, check with a used-car dealer, the used-car ads in your newspaper, or the *National Automobile Dealers Association Blue Book* (http://www.kbb.com, http://www.kelleybluebook, or http://www.edmunds. com) to see what your car's model and year is now worth. Bring any rare coins or stamps into a reputable dealer for an appraisal. For antiques or other collectibles, contact a local member of the American Society of Appraisers, found in the Yellow Pages or have a look at eBay (http://www.ebay.com).

The Low Road: Tallying Up Your Liabilities

Liabilities should be divided into short- and long-term categories, just as assets are. That's because some debts you need to pay back very soon, like current bills or credit cards, whereas other debts, such as mortgages or college loans, will take years to repay. Roadmap 2.2 is a Liabilities Worksheet to help you list to whom you owe money, the interest rate you are paying, if any, when the loan comes due if there is such a maturity date, and how much money you owe.

If your financial situation is simpler than the worksheets in Roadmaps 2.1 and 2.2, Roadmap 2.3 offers a briefer version that should be easier for you to use.

When completing the worksheet in Roadmap 2.2, use the following four main categories for listing your liabilities:

Liabilities Worksheet

Liabilities	To Whom	Interest Rate %	Due Date	Total Balance Due $
1. Current Liabilities				
Alimony		_____ %		$ _____
Bills				
Electric & Gas				
Home Contractor				
Oil Company				
Physician & Dentist				
Retail Stores				
Telephone				
Other				
Child Support				
Loans to Individuals				
Total Current Liabilities				$ _____
2. Unpaid Taxes				
Income Taxes				
Federal		_____ %		$ _____
State				
City				
Capital Gains Taxes				
Federal				
State				
City				
Property Taxes				
Sales Taxes Locality				
Social Security Taxes (self-employed)				
Total Unpaid Taxes				$ _____
3. Real Estate Liabilities				
Home #1				
First Mortgage		_____ %		$ _____
Second Mortgage				
Home Equity Loan				
Home #2				
First Mortgage				
Second Mortgage				
Home Equity Loan				
Rental Property				
First Mortgage				
Second Mortgage				
Total Real Estate Liabilities				$ _____

Roadmap 2.2 (continued)

Liabilities Worksheet

Liabilities	To Whom	Interest Rate %	Due Date	Total Balance Due $
4. Installment Liabilities				
Automobile Loans	_____	_____%	_____	$_____
Bill Consolidation Loans	_____	_____	_____	_____
Credit Cards	_____	_____	_____	_____
Education Loans	_____	_____	_____	_____
Equipment and Appliance Loans	_____	_____	_____	_____
Furniture Loans	_____	_____	_____	_____
Home Improvement Loans	_____	_____	_____	_____
Liability Judgments	_____	_____	_____	_____
Life Insurance Loans	_____	_____	_____	_____
Margin Loans Against Securities	_____	_____	_____	_____
Overdraft Bank Loans	_____	_____	_____	_____
Retirement Plan Loans	_____	_____	_____	_____
Total Installment Liabilities				$_____
Total Liabilities				$_____

Current liabilities. These are debts you must pay within the next six months. In this category would be bills from the utilities (i.e., the telephone company, the electric company, the gas company, and the oil company), physicians and dentists, home repair contractors, and other short-term creditors. You should also include regular alimony or child support payments if these apply to you. If you owe money to a relative or friend who helped you out in a pinch, make sure to include that debt as well in this category.

Unpaid taxes. These taxes might be due either on April 15 or as part of your quarterly estimated tax payments to both the IRS and your state tax department. They include not only income taxes but also the capital gains taxes you owe on an asset you have sold for a profit. You should also include local property taxes, which you may have to pay directly, or which may be paid by the company that holds your mortgage. Finally, if you are self-employed, you must make sure to account for Social Security self-employment taxes due.

Real estate debt. This category of debt includes both first and second mortgages on your primary residence and on any second (or additional) homes you may have. It also includes any mortgages you owe on rental properties that are producing income. On a separate line, list any home equity loans outstanding on your home(s).

Installment debt. Installment debt covers all loans you have committed to pay off over a period of time. This category includes automobile loans from either a car dealer or a bank; loans taken out to consolidate bills or for any other purpose including overdraft loans attached to your checking account; education loans from your college or university; loans to pay for equipment or appliances, including computers; furniture loans; home improvement loans; life insurance loans taken against the cash value in your policies; and margin loans from a brokerage house taken against the value of your securities. If you have lost a lawsuit and there is a liability judgment against you, that should be considered part of the installment debt you owe.

Finally, if you have borrowed against your retirement plan at work, which is usually some form of salary reduction plan, you normally are obligated to pay it back by payroll deduction over five years. This obligation should also be counted as installment debt. Credit card charges from MasterCard, Visa, American Express, Diners Club, Discover, as well as retail stores, on which you owe at least the minimum payment or where purchase was at 0 percent for an initial payment period and interest will begin accruing, should also be noted in this category because you control when to pay off the outstanding balance.

Stop and Look at Your Map

Now, for the moment of truth: Take your total assets from the Assets Worksheet in Roadmap 2.1 and subtract your total liabilities from the Liabilities Worksheet in Roadmap 2.2. This determines your net worth:

Total Assets	$ _____
(Minus) Total Liabilities	(_____)
Equals Positive (or Negative) Net Worth	$ _____

(If you used the simpler version in Roadmap 2.3, you've already done this.)

Roadmap 2.3

Simple Net Worth Statement

Assets: What You Own	Amount $
Cash: On Hand	
Checking Accounts	
Savings Accounts	
Money Markets	
Other	
Real Estate/Property:	
Principal Residence	
Second Residence	
Land	
Income Property	
Other	
Investments (Market Value):	
Cash Value Life Insurance	
Certificates of Deposit	
U.S. Treasury Bills/Savings Bonds	
Stocks	
Bonds	
Mutual Funds	
Limited Partnerships	
Annuities	
IRA–Regular/Roth/Keogh Plan	
401(k), 403(b), or 457 Plans	
Pension Plan/Retirement Plans	
Other	
Personal Loans Receivable	
Personal Property (Present Value):	
Automobiles, Vehicles	
Recreational Vehicle/Boat	
Electronic Equipment	
Home Furnishings	
Home Entertainment Equipment	

Appliances and Furniture	_____
Collectibles/Antiques	_____
Jewelry and Furs	_____
Other	_____
Total Assets	_____

Liabilities: What You Owe	**Amount $**
Current Debts:	
Household	_____
Medical	_____
Credit Cards	_____
Department Store Cards	_____
Back Taxes	_____
Legal	_____
Child Support	_____
Alimony	_____
Other	_____
Mortgages:	
Principal Residence	_____
Second Residence	_____
Land	_____
Income Property	_____
Other	_____
Loans:	
Home Equity	_____
Bank/Finance Company	_____
Bank/Finance Company	_____
Automobiles, Vehicles	_____
Recreational Vehicle/Boat	_____
Education/Student	_____
Life Insurance	_____
Personal (from family or friends)	_____
Retirement Accounts	_____
Other	_____
Total Liabilities	_____
Total Assets − Total Liabilities = Net Worth	_____

First, notice whether your net worth is positive or negative. If it's positive, you've probably been doing a good job at building assets and keeping liabilities under control. Now that you know where you stand, you are in a good position to see your net worth grow even more in the coming years, which should give you some comfort and peace of mind.

Even if your net worth is negative, don't despair. You've just discovered something very important about your finances. Assessing your financial situation realistically is the first step toward getting out of trouble. Clearly, you have too much debt for the amount of assets you have accumulated. Remember, this is only a snapshot of your current situation. Let's hope the next time you calculate your net worth, it will be a more positive experience. And we'll help you, in the rest of this book, to improve your financial situation.

You should calculate your net worth each year, and compare it to your calculations for the past five years to see how you have been progressing. Use the simple form in Roadmap 2.4 to keep records.

▶ On and Off Ramps: Analyzing Your Cash Flow (Your Income and Current Expenses)

Now that you know how much you really have, you should also do a detailed analysis of where your money is coming from and where it is being spent. This is known in the financial planning world as a *cash flow analysis* because it allows you to trace your sources and uses of money. If you are feeling overwhelmed, take a break and come back to this another day. But it's important to do a cash flow analysis, because it differs from the assessment of your assets and liabilities, which (as we've said) are a *snapshot* in time. In contrast, your cash flow is constantly changing, depending on how much income you're receiving and how much you're spending—both of which you should have more immediate control over than your assets and liabilities, unless you decide, for example, to sell your house or other assets. At this point, though, you may not want to have to make any major decisions like that, so let's just proceed with looking at where your money is coming from and going.

Even though analyzing cash flow is a simple exercise, most people never do it. They wonder, "Where did all my money go?" at the end of each month and anxiously wait for their next paycheck to pay their bills. By doing the cash flow analysis in this section, you will never again have to be one of those people, because even if you are anxious for each paycheck, you will know exactly

Roadmap 2.4

Net Worth Comparison, Year to Year

Year	Net Worth	Percentage Increase/Decrease
This year	_____	
Last year	_____	_____
Two years ago	_____	_____
Three years ago	_____	_____
Four years ago	_____	_____
Five years ago	_____	_____

how much income you can expect to receive as well as nearly all the expenses you plan to cover with that income. (Also, you shouldn't really plan on any sudden windfalls, even if your spouse's insurance money or other funds are coming from the estate, but you should expect a few surprise expenses. Once you've actually *received* any funds from your spouse's estate, then you can revise your cash flow analysis and your net worth statements. You may have estimated this once you knew the estimated value of your spouse's estate; if that is the case, revise it if necessary based on actual receipts.)

The cash flow worksheet presented in Roadmap 2.5 is designed to be used on an annual basis. You may receive some of your income, such as bonuses or capital gains distributions made by mutual funds, only at certain times of the year—for example, in December. Similarly, many of your expenses, such as tuition payments, fuel oil bills, or quarterly tax bills, occur only during certain months of the year. By totaling all your annual income and expenses, you will get a sense of how your overall cash flow looks for the year.

It is also important to do a more short-term cash flow analysis because sometimes you can be caught in a cash squeeze when your expenses are due much before the income arrives. You can use the cash flow worksheet in Roadmap 2.5 on both a monthly and a quarterly basis.

ave designed this Roadmap to be as comprehensive as possible, providing you with lines for the most common sources of income and the most frequent expenses, broken down into familiar categories. If you currently do not have one of the sources of income listed, leave the lines blank. The same holds true on the expense side. If you are not spending money for day care or a health club membership, leave it blank. The best way to complete this Roadmap is to take your bank, brokerage, insurance, and other statements and last year's tax return, along with your last year-end paycheck and other records you have accumulated for the past six months, and fill in the real numbers. (Fortunately, you've already gathered all these forms while you read Chapter 1.) Note: As you complete the Roadmap, remember to exclude any income or expenses that you will no longer have.

This is not an exercise in wishful thinking; this is a document that will show you, for better or worse, how you actually are earning and spending your money now. It's no use inflating the income and low-balling the expenses because you're the only one who will be hurt by not knowing the truth. You don't have to show the results to anyone; this is only for you.

Sources of Income. The income side of the cash flow worksheet in Roadmap 2.5 is broken into six categories: earned, self-employment, family, government, retirement, and investment income. The following sections offer a brief guide to what kinds of income fall into each category. (For each of the six categories, we have provided a line on the Roadmap to subtotal the income, which will make it easier to add up your total income at the end.)

Earned income. The most common and largest source of income for most people, of course, is their salary from a job. You should note on the Roadmap your net take-home pay, after deductions. Other sources of earned income include commissions paid to salespeople, bonuses for extraordinary performance, overtime, and tips. You may also be entitled to stock options. There are also many forms of deferred compensation that can be paid out to you, based on your performance or in accordance with the provisions of a contract. If you expect to exercise stock options or receive deferred compensation in the next year, you should note this on the Roadmap.

Self-employment income. If you work for yourself or a closely held partnership, most of your income will come from this income category. Because taxes or other deductions are not normally withheld from self-employment income, you will have to pay income and self-employment taxes on this money on, at least, a quarterly basis through estimated tax filings.

Family income. If you happen to come from a family that has put money in a trust for you, this can be a significant source of regular income now and in the future. On the Roadmap you should list the income produced from the assets you inherited or the assets in a trust for you. If you receive regular gifts from family members, the total amount should also be listed here.

Government income. You might qualify to receive regular checks from the federal or state government. If your other income is low enough, you can get welfare or Aid to Families with Dependent Children (AFDC) funds. If you have a disability caused by an accident or illness, you may qualify for disability insurance and/or workers' compensation insurance. If you had a job, but were laid off, you are entitled to unemployment insurance for several months. Note these amounts on the Roadmap.

Retirement income. There are several sources of income once you have retired, assuming you have been building up retirement assets for most of your working life. You can receive a monthly payment from an annuity, issued by an insurance company, based on your contributions to the annuity over time. Alternatively, you can take the lump sum you receive from your employer once you retire and buy an annuity from an insurance company to ensure a fixed monthly income for the rest of your life. You may have accumulated monthly pension benefits. Similarly, starting at age 59½, you can take money out of your IRA or Keogh account without penalty. (You must pay a 10 percent penalty if you withdraw from these accounts sooner.) If you worked at a company that offered a profit-sharing plan, a 401(k) or 403(b) plan, or a pension plan, you can have the earnings paid to you in monthly installments. Finally, you may be entitled to survivor's and/or retirements benefits from Social Security. (Note: If your spouse earned more money than you did and/or worked for a longer period of time, you may be better off collecting a portion of your spouse's benefits than collecting in your own right. Before you apply, check with your Social Security office.)

In addition to your own projected retirement benefits, when you lose your spouse, your spouse's employer may be an important source of financial support. If the employee benefits department has not yet been notified of your spouse's passing, write a letter informing the department of the date your spouse died (include his or her Social Security number). Request information about the benefits you should expect to receive and what steps you must take.

In most companies, employees are covered by term life insurance amounting to at least one year's salary or, in many cases, double one year's wages. Therefore, if your spouse earned $50,000 annually, you might be eligible for a death benefit of $100,000. In addition to term life insurance, many companies offer an *accidental death benefit policy,* which pays you a lump sum if your spouse died while traveling on company business.

Many employers also provide a *survivor income plan.* Such a policy pays a regular monthly income to widows or widowers and their dependents who counted on the income generated by the deceased spouse. Benefits are based on a percentage of the worker's salary with a spouse getting up to 30 percent of the employee's pay and children receiving an additional 20 percent. For young children, the plan may pay benefits for as long as 20 years, depending on their needs. However, if you remarry, they usually, but not always, cease. Survivor income plans are designed to supplement Social Security survivor's benefits.

Depending on the employer's benefits plan, you may be eligible to receive retirement benefits based on defined benefit and defined contribution plans if your spouse was vested at the time of death. Your spouse may have worked at several companies and become vested in many retirement plans during the working life, so contact *all* past employers, as well as the current employer, and inquire about retirement benefits.

You must choose between receiving the value of a pension in a lump sum or as an annuity in monthly installments for the rest of your life. If you feel able to do better by investing the money yourself, take the lump sum and invest in a diversified portfolio of stocks, bonds, and mutual funds that will provide for your needs. However, if you have little confidence in the stock market or in your investing ability, opt for the monthly payments, which will relieve you of the responsibility of investing the money and which will ensure stable income for life. (Again, we'll discuss investments in more detail in Chapter 5.)

You and your family also are eligible to continue coverage under your spouse's health insurance plan for three years at the same price the employer would have paid, plus a small administrative fee. This continuation is guaranteed under the federal Congressional Omnibus Budget Reconciliation Act (COBRA). You will have to pay premiums, which you might not have paid when your spouse was alive; however, you will receive group insurance rates. These generally will be far lower for the same type of coverage than you could qualify for as an individual.

Investment income. This category offers the most possibilities because there are so many kinds of bank instruments, bonds, stocks, mutual funds, and limited partnerships designed to throw off income. (We'll discuss how to maximize these investments in Chapter 5; for now, you just want to list what you currently have.)

Among bank products, you can earn regular interest income from certificates of deposit (CDs), money-market deposit accounts, and other savings and checking accounts. The two additional kinds of short-term interest-bearing accounts are money-market mutual funds, which come in both taxable and tax-exempt varieties, and Treasury bills, which come in three-month, six-month, and one-year maturities.

Among income-producing bonds, your options include:

- ► corporate bonds (issued by corporations);
- ► convertible bonds (also issued by companies, but with the added option of converting the bonds into company stock in the future);
- ► Treasury notes maturing in up to 10 years and Treasury bonds coming due in up to 30 years;
- ► municipal bonds (issued by states and localities and paying interest free from federal and usually state taxes); and
- ► foreign bonds (issued by non-U.S. corporations or foreign governments).

In addition, you may be counting on income produced from selling any of these kinds of bonds for a profit, listed on the Roadmap as capital gains from bond sales. Similarly, you can produce regular income by investing in bond mutual funds that buy any of these taxable or tax-exempt bonds. Stocks also give you several options for producing regular income. Many individual stocks pay quarterly dividends, with some, like public utilities, yielding 5 percent or more. Many mutual funds investing in stocks are also designed to pay a significant monthly dividend to income-oriented investors. Plus, most mutual funds make a yearly payout of all the capital gains they have accumulated during the year, known as a capital gains distribution. If you plan to sell some of your stocks or stock funds to realize a profit, that should be entered on the Roadmap as income from capital gains.

If you have any interests in such partnerships, enter the annual income you expect from them on the Roadmap. Next, total the income you expect to receive in all six categories, and add any other income sources as well, to create your grand total: annual income.

Expenses. Now you're going to figure out where all your income goes every year. Your expenses can be divided roughly into two categories: what is *fixed*, meaning it must be paid on an annual or a monthly basis, and what is *flexible*, meaning you have more control over whether and when you spend it. By filling out the expense portion of the roadmap in these two categories, you will be able to see what percentage of your income is taken up by fixed expenses. This will give you a clearer idea of how much money you have left over for discretionary spending. There are seven categories that should be considered *fixed expenses*: automobile-related expenses, family expenses, home-related expenses, insurance, savings and investments, taxes, and utilities.

Automobile-related expenses. Most people either lease their car from the dealer or buy it with an auto loan. In either case, you will have to make a monthly payment until the lease is up or the loan is paid off. To keep the car running, of course, you will need gasoline in the tank and oil under the hood.

Family expenses. If you have children who go to a school that charges tuition, this also goes into the fixed expenses column.

Home-related expenses. Whether you own or rent, certain expenses are impossible to avoid. Owners must make their monthly mortgage payments, just as renters must pay the rent every month. And if you have cable television or Internet service, make an allowance in your budget for those charges.

Utilities. Don't forget to include your electric utility bill, the cost of gas or oil, and your telephone bill. In some places, you are also charged for water or sewage service.

Insurance. Until you have a claim, paying the insurance company never feels like a good use of money. But when you actually have to make a claim, you are relieved that you kept up with your premiums. The most common forms of insurance you will have to pay are auto, disability, dental, liability, health, homeowners, and life insurance. We hope your spouse had adequate life insurance, because that money will be helpful in the coming months and years. To protect yourself and your heirs in the future, make sure you continue to pay your other insurance premiums. (These are all discussed in more detail in Chapter 4.)

Savings and investments. At last, here is an expense category that lets you feel you are not spending money you will never see again. It may seem hard to think of saving and investing as fixed expenses, but it's the best way to accumulate funds. The easiest way to invest is through some kind of automatic savings plan, such as your salary reduction plan (called a 401(k) in companies, a 403(b) in nonprofit institutions, and a 457 in government agencies).

You can also save at your bank by building up your emergency fund, which should be kept with at least three to six months' worth of expenses in reserve, if possible. Such a fund is crucial if you suddenly become unemployed, must pay for a major auto or house repair, or have a major medical emergency. And even though you may not think of repaying debt as savings, it's one of the best savings moves you can make. Not many investments out there can guarantee you, for example, the instant 18+ percent after tax return you earn when you pay off credit card debt.

Taxes. If you do not have enough money for taxes withheld from your paycheck or you have a great deal of self-employment income, you must make quarterly estimated payments to both the IRS and your state. Also, the self-employed should make regular Social Security self-employment tax payments as well. If you own your home, your city or town government expects you to pay property taxes, though often those taxes are actually paid on your behalf by the bank that holds your mortgage and has set up your tax escrow account.

These seven categories include most of what you absolutely have to pay every year. Nearly 70 percent of a typical American's income is spent on fixed expenses.

With some good planning, you will have about 30 percent of your income left for more discretionary purchases we will refer to as *flexible spending*. There are many more ways to spend money when you have some choice in the matter. We have broken flexible expenses into 13 categories: children, clothing, contributions and dues, education, equipment and vehicles, financial and professional services, food, home maintenance, medical care, miscellaneous, recreation and entertainment, savings and investments, and travel and vacations.

Children. If you have children, you know that the joys of parenthood don't come cheap. As children grow up, what they require and desire changes, and it usually gets more expensive. While your infant may be perfectly content with a pacifier for $.69, your teenager may not be satisfied with anything but the latest stereo equipment, starting at roughly $500. Many older children, even those who have graduated from college, often continue to need financial help (and often housing) until they get a job and settle down in life.

Clothing. You probably will need to augment your clothing budget if you were a stay-at-home mom or dad, and are returning to work in a professional setting, where appearance is important. Set aside money not only for new clothes and shoes but also for the upkeep of your clothes, such as for dry cleaning, tailoring, and pressing. All those trips to the dry cleaner may seem insignificant, but those bills can really add up over a year.

Contributions, dues, and gifts. The amount you give to charities, religious institutions, and political candidates is up to you. You may be able to deduct some or all of your contributions, which will give you a bit of a tax break. For the most part, though, give because you believe in the cause, not to get the write-off. If you are a member of a union, dues are deductible. And gift giving can always take a big bite out of your budget because you can get carried away with your feelings of generosity toward the recipients.

Education. If you or your children plan on going to a school that charges tuition, it's never too early to start budgeting. Remember, you will have to pay not only for tuition but also room and board, books, software, and supplies. If your children take lessons for anything from violin to karate, don't forget to budget for them.

Equipment and vehicles. Every time you buy a new vehicle or piece of equipment to make your life easier or pleasanter, you are adding potential expenses. Cars, boats, motorcycles, and motor homes all need maintenance, insurance, registrations, licenses, and a place to park.

When you lose your spouse and you both had cars, you may find you don't need one and decide to sell it.

If you want to trade in your existing car for a new one, you may have trouble leasing or qualifying for an auto loan if you have not established a credit history and earned income of your own. Such leases and loans are granted based on a strong credit history and record of steady income. If your spouse was the only one to create such a history, your credit request may be denied. One of the biggest problems facing widows and widowers is that they often have not established their own credit histories and records of earnings, which lenders use to assess their ability to repay debts.

In addition to cars, your televisions, recorders, stereos, CD players, and other consumer electronics need DVDs and CDs, along with occasional repairs. The same holds true for all of life's other conveniences, from Cuisinarts to washing machines. So be wary of making lots of new expenditures at this time.

Financial and professional services. Some areas of finance are too complicated for the average person, and it is worthwhile to pay an expert for advice. That can be particularly true with tax, legal, and investment matters (which we'll discuss in Chapters 3 and 5). Also, most of the time, you are charged fees to make financial transactions, from the pesky fees that banks charge to use automatic teller machines to brokerage fees you pay to buy or sell stocks or mutual funds. Some of these fees can be avoided; for example, you can buy a no-load mutual fund directly from a fund company or discount broker that does not charge a commission. Still, even no-load funds charge an annual management fee, which is taken out of your fund's return. If the advice you get from financial professionals is solid, the charges can be well worth it.

Most advisors are compensated at least in part by the commissions you pay when you buy an investment or insurance product they sell. If the advice is biased in favor of the advisor, or you don't act on it because you don't understand the advice or you think it is inappropriate for you, the commissions you pay can be a major money-waster. Other advisors charge by the hour or for a project and receive no compensation from any other source. This compensation structure removes many of these inherent conflicts of interest.

Food. In addition to the food you buy to serve at home, you should allow for food outside the home, including both restaurant meals and on-the-fly snacks. Count any purchases of alcohol and tobacco in this food category.

Home maintenance. The bigger and/or older your house or apartment, the more expensive it is to maintain. You should expect a certain amount of repairs every year, along with ongoing cleaning and household expenses, from soap to dishes to light bulbs. Remember the fees for outside maintenance as well, which include removing the garbage and snow and tending the lawn and garden. If you have a home office, you will have to keep it stocked with file folders, pens, and probably computer supplies and fax paper. If you have suffered a break-in or damage to your house that is not covered by your insurance policy, you should count that, too.

Medical care. Even employees with health insurance through their employers usually bear more and more medical costs these days. Often, employees have to pay part of the insurance premium, deductibles, and co-payments, as well as for drugs, eyeglasses, and medical devices like wheelchairs and canes. In some cases, insurance companies limit the amount of a physician's, dentist's or hospital's bill that they will reimburse, leaving the insured to pay for the remainder. In addition, you must budget to cover over-the-counter medicines, personal care items, and toiletries, as well as haircuts, manicures and pedicures, if they are part of your routine. You may also have to pick up medical expenses for your older parents if they do not have enough money, whether they live on their own, with you, or in a nursing home, because most insurance will not cover all of their expenses.

Miscellaneous. There are always going to be some expenses that just don't fit into any of the other categories. Un-reimbursed business expenses and postage are two that come to mind. Then there are the *recurring miscellaneous expense* hits. Generally each of these expenses happens only once, but a new one seems to occur every month or so. One month, the boiler breaks down, the next month, your parked car is hit, but the damage is just under your insurance deductible. By assuming such recurring miscellaneous expenses will pop up, you can budget for them. And then there is always that big hole in your budget we like to call "mystery cash." You had cash in your wallet, and you have absolutely no idea what you spent it on by the end of the week. Try writing down what you spend every penny on during one week, and you might be able to unlock the secrets of mystery cash.

Recreation and entertainment. Most people can't exist without some kind of hobby, sport, or recreation. You may like pets, books, movies, music, photography, plays, sporting events, videos, or dining out, all of which can become expensive activities. You may be committed to your health, having joined a fitness club or playing a sport like golf, where greens fees are required. Nothing is wrong with any of these—except that they don't come free and they may not fit within your new spending plan or budget.

Savings and investments. Although you should put aside a certain amount of money as part of your fixed expenses to keep your emergency fund solvent, you should also try to invest in bank instruments, stocks, bonds, and mutual funds that will provide you with the wherewithal to reach your financial goals. If you don't start investing for these goals, the money will never be there when you need it, whether it is for your child's college education or your retirement. Although some of the investments should be in a regular taxable bank, brokerage, or mutual fund account, some of the money should be compounding tax deferred in an IRA, 401(k), or a Keogh account.

Travel and vacations. There are two kinds of travel—for business and for pleasure. You should set aside money for both—even though taking a vacation may seem like the last thing you'd want to do right now, you may want to get away for a few days or weeks or visit family or faraway friends. Vacations can be wonderfully relaxing but somehow they can end up costing more than you expect. You should be realistic about the cost of airfares, hotels, car rentals, food, tips, even souvenirs.

If you work, you will need to spend money to commute to work, whether that means driving (paying tolls and parking your car) or taking a bus, subway, or train. In addition, there are often expenses you incur while on the road for your business that your company might not reimburse, like watching a pay-per-view movie in your hotel room.

So, there you have it—the 13 major categories on which you spend your money. As you fill out the cash flow worksheet in Roadmap 2.5, only certain sections may apply to you right now. Some day, you will probably use those sections you cannot use now. For the moment, just skip those categories that do not apply. Your life is in flux, so your financial situation will probably change, too.

After you've filled out both the income and expense sides of this Roadmap, it will be time to get down to the bottom line. Subtract your expenses from your income, and you have your annual cash flow. If you are taking in more than you are spending, congratulations. You are in *positive cash flow*. Your next job is to figure out the best places for your extra cash—probably savings vehicles and investments.

If, on the other hand, your expenses total more than your income—not an unlikely situation—you are in *negative cash flow,* and it's time to start scrutinizing your expenses. Just because you have negative cash flow does not mean you are in bad trouble. For example, you may still be putting away money in your company savings plan, which means you are investing more than you remember. On the other hand, if the reason you are spending more than you are taking in is causing you to spend down savings or go into debt, it's time to take notice.

Roadmap 2.5

Cash Flow Worksheet

Annual Income	$ Amount	$ Total
1. Earned Income		
Salary after Deductions	$_____	
Bonuses	_____	
Commissions	_____	
Deferred Compensation	_____	
Overtime	_____	
Stock Options	_____	
Tips	_____	
Other	_____	
Total Earned Income		$_____
2. Self-Employment Income		
Freelance Income	$_____	
Income from Partnerships	_____	
Income from Running a Small Business	_____	
Rental Income from Real Estate	_____	
Royalties	_____	
Other	_____	
Total Self-employment Income		$_____
3. Family Income		
Alimony Income	$_____	
Child Support Income	_____	
Family Trust Income	_____	
Gifts from Family Members	_____	
Inheritance Income	_____	
Other	_____	
Total Family Income		$_____
4. Government Income		
Aid to Families with Dependent Children Income	$_____	
Disability Insurance Income	_____	
Unemployment Insurance Income	_____	
Veterans Benefits	_____	
Welfare Income	_____	
Workers' Compensation Income	_____	

Other _____

Total Government Income $_____

5. Retirement Income

Annuity Payments $_____

Social Security Income _____

Pension Income _____

Income from IRAs _____

Income from Keogh Accounts _____

Income from Profit-Sharing Accounts _____

Income from Salary Reduction Plans _____

(401(k), 403(b), 457 plans)

Other _____

Total Retirement Income $_____

6. Investment Income

Bank Account Interest

CDs $_____

Money-Market Accounts _____

NOW Accounts _____

Saving Accounts _____

Bonds and Bond Funds

Capital Gains _____

Dividends _____

Interest _____

Other _____

Limited Partnerships (real estate,

oil, gas) _____

Money Funds and T-Bills

Taxable Funds _____

Tax-Exempt Funds _____

T-Bills _____

Stock and Stock Funds

Capital Gains _____

Dividends _____

Interest _____

Other _____

Other _____

Total Investment Income $_____

7. Other Income (specify)

_____ $_____

Total Other Income $_____

Total Annual Income $_____

Annual Expenses	$ Amount	$ Total
1. Fixed Expenses		
Automobile-Related	$_____	
Car Payment (loan or lease)	_____	
Gasoline or Oil	_____	
Other	_____	
Total		$_____
Family		
Alimony	_____	
Child Support Payments	_____	
Food and Beverage	_____	
School Tuition	_____	
Other	_____	
Total		$_____
Home-Related		
Mortgage Payments #1	_____	
Mortgage Payments #2	_____	
Rent	_____	
Total		$_____
Insurance		
Auto	_____	
Disability	_____	
Dental	_____	
Health	_____	
Homeowners	_____	
Life	_____	
Other	_____	
Total		$_____
Savings, Investments, and Loans		
Bank Loan Repayment	_____	
Emergency Fund Contributions	_____	
Salary Reduction Plans		
Contributions (401(k), 403(b), 457 plans)	_____	
Other	_____	
Total		$_____
Taxes		
Federal	_____	
Local	_____	
Property	_____	
Social Security (self-employed)	_____	
State	_____	

Other	_____	
Total		$ _____
Utilities		
Electricity	_____	
Gas	_____	
Telephone	_____	
Water and Sewage	_____	
Cable Television	_____	
Other	_____	
Total		$ _____
Other (specify)		
_____	_____	
Total		$ _____
Total Fixed Expenses		$ _____

2. Flexible Expenses

Children		
Allowances	$ _____	
Babysitting	_____	
Books	_____	
Camp Fees	_____	
Day Care	_____	
Events (parties, class trips, etc.)	_____	
Toys	_____	
Other	_____	
Total		$ _____
Clothing		
New Purchases	_____	
Shoes	_____	
Upkeep (cleaning, tailoring, dry cleaning, etc.)	_____	
Total		$ _____
Contributions and Dues		
Charitable Donations	_____	
Gifts (Christmas, birthdays, etc.)	_____	
Political Contributions	_____	
Religious Contributions	_____	
Union Dues	_____	
Other	_____	
Total		$ _____
Education		
Room and Board	_____	

Annual Expenses	$ Amount	$ Total
Books and Supplies (parents and/or children)	_____	
Tuition (parents and/or children)	_____	
Other	_____	
Total		$_____
Equipment and Vehicles		
Appliance Purchases and Maintenance	_____	
Car, Boat, and Other Vehicle Purchases and Maintenance	_____	
Computer Purchases, etc.	_____	
Consumer Electronics Purchases	_____	
Licenses and Registration of Cars, Boats, etc.	_____	
Parking	_____	
Other	_____	
Total		$_____
Financial and Professional Services		
Banking Fees	_____	
Brokerage Commissions and Fees	_____	
Financial Advice	_____	
Legal Advice	_____	
Tax Preparation Fees	_____	
Other	_____	
Total		$_____
Food		
Alcohol	_____	
Foods and Snacks at Home	_____	
Restaurant Meals and Snacks	_____	
Tobacco	_____	
Other	_____	
Total		$_____
Home Maintenance		
Garbage Removal	_____	
Garden Supplies and Maintenance	_____	
Home Office Supplies	_____	
Home Furnishings	_____	
Home or Apartment Repairs and Renovations	_____	
Home Cleaning Services	_____	
Home Supplies	_____	
Lawn Care and Snow Removal	_____	

Linens _____

Uninsured Casualty or Theft Loss _____

Other _____

Total $_____

Medical Care

Dental Care _____

Drugs (over the counter) _____

Drugs (prescriptions) _____

Eye care and Eyeglasses _____

Hospital (uninsured portion) _____

Medical Devices (wheelchairs,
canes, etc.) _____

Medical Expenses (parents, etc.) _____

Nursing Home Fees (parents, etc.) _____

Personal Beauty Care (hair stylist,
manicurist, etc.) _____

Personal Care (cosmetics,
toiletries, etc.) _____

Physician Bills _____

Unreimbursed Medical Expenses _____

Other _____

Total $_____

Miscellaneous

Mystery Cash _____

Postage and Stamps _____

Recurring Nonrecurring Expenses _____

Unreimbursed Business Expenses _____

Other _____

Total $_____

Recreation and Entertainment

Animal Care _____

Books _____

Club Dues _____

Cultural Events _____

Health Club Memberships _____

Hobbies _____

Lottery Tickets _____

Magazine and Newspaper
Subscriptions _____

Movie Admissions _____

Music Admissions _____

Photography (cameras,
developing, film, etc.) _____

Play Admissions _____

Annual Expenses	$ Amount	$ Total
Recreational Equipment (games, sports, etc.)	_____	
Sporting Events Admission	_____	
Videotape Rentals	_____	
Other	_____	
Total		$_____
Savings and Investments		
Bank Savings Contributions	_____	
Stock, Bond, and Mutual Fund Contributions	_____	
IRA Contributions	_____	
Keogh Account Contributions	_____	
401(k)/403(b)	_____	
Other	_____	
Total		$_____
Travel and Vacations		
Bus Fares	_____	
Subway Costs	_____	
Tolls	_____	
Train Fares	_____	
Travel Expenses (other than vacations)	_____	
Unreimbursed Business Travel Expenses	_____	
Vacations (airfare)	_____	
Vacations (car rental)	_____	
Vacations (food)	_____	
Vacations (hotel)	_____	
Vacations (other)	_____	
Other	_____	
Total		$_____
Other (specify)		
_____	_____	
Total		$_____
Total Flexible Expenses		$_____
Total Annual Expenses (Fixed + Flexible)		$_____
Total Annual Income (Minus)		$_____
Total Annual Expenses (Equals)		(_____)
Total Net Annual Positive (Or Negative) Cash Flow		$_____

▶ Start Your Engine: Where Are You Going?

If your spouse handled all your financial matters, you may be new to budgeting. After all, now is not a time when you want to be worrying about having enough money to pay the bills and to buy and do the things you need to do in the months ahead. Most financial experts agree that writing everything down and seeing the total picture will help you make your plans and spend your money wisely. Still, if you're feeling overwhelmed by all the financial analysis you've done so far in this chapter, come back to this another day and start fresh.

Plan the Road Ahead: Create Your Annual Budget

A *yearly budget worksheet,* which lists non-monthly anticipated expenses (shown in Roadmap 2.6) seems to make all the difference in the world for people, right from the beginning. By starting with this overall annual picture of where your money goes, above and beyond your regular monthly bills and expenses, you can see immediately where you stand each month.

A yearly budget worksheet is designed to give you a general annual overview of your *irregular, occasional, non-monthly,* and *periodic* expenses at a glance. This method often provides a more manageable approach than the use of files, notes on the calendar, or even some software programs.

Having this information can prevent those times when after you've finally paid all the bills and heaved a sigh of relief, the next day you find yourself deluged with auto insurance and property tax bills you had overlooked or not anticipated. All this can put your whole budget in a tailspin once again. Be careful.

By having all this information as early in the year as possible, you can use it to make necessary arrangements ahead of time. How much money should you put aside in your reserve savings account for dental work, could you postpone getting a new sofa, how can a vacation be less costly, is it time to cut back on gifts? By thinking these options through ahead of time and taking action, you won't be falling back on savings, credit cards, or loans to get you through the year.

Be patient as you go through this first form. Initially, it will require more time. However, the insights and information you gain will be well worth your time. Once you complete Roadmap 2.6, it becomes a valuable reference for the remainder of the year.

Yearly Budget Worksheet

Year 20____

(Non-Monthly Anticipated Expenses)

FIXED AND ESTIMATED NON-MONTHLY EXPENSES

		JAN	FEB	MAR	APR	MAY	JUNE	JULY	AUG	SEPT	OCT	NOV	DEC	TOTAL	MO. AVG.
Housing	Property Tax/ Homeowners Insurance														
	Home/Yard Maintenance														
	Utilities														
Transportation	Auto Insurance														
	Auto Expenses														
Health	Insurance— Other														
	Medical Expenses														
	Dental/Vision Expenses														

Additional Non-Monthly Expenses																
Dues/Fees																
Education/Tuition																
Clothing																
Recreation																
Vacation/Trips																
Gifts—Birthday																
Gifts—Other																
Holiday Events																
Children's Activities																
Pets																
Total																

Reserve Savings: $_____

Total Expenses $_____ ÷ 12 = $_____ /Month

To get started, grab your pencil, eraser, and calculator. Then gather up your checkbook registers, insurance papers, investment and credit card statements, paycheck stubs, and any other related household papers that may give the exact or estimated amounts of expenses plus the months these expenses are due or paid. (Again, you should already have these in one place, from the organization you did in Chapter 1.)

Start at the top left of the worksheet in Roadmap 2.6. Look at the expense category and, if it applies to you, move across the page to the right and fill in the exact or estimated amount under the month or months the expense is due. Use a pencil because as you work this through, changes and new additions will definitely come up.

See the suggestion list in Roadmap 2.7 to find additional and often overlooked expenses that may apply to your household but are not on this worksheet. Roadmap 2.6 is deliberately kept generic so you can adjust it to your own unique needs.

For those expense categories where you really don't have a clue what the cost will be, hazard a guess. That's right. It is okay not to be perfect and it is also more valuable to keep moving through this exercise than to use the missing information as a reason to stop or get discouraged. You are already going through the most important process by thinking about these expenses and filling in most of the information. You can always add to this section later as new or more accurate information becomes available.

Roadmap 2.6 is a guideline for you. You may find you have to add or cross out and replace certain categories. Remember to do whatever works best for your unique financial picture.

Your yearly budget worksheet will be especially helpful if you are on a very tight budget this year. Some of your expenses, like insurance or taxes, will be fixed, and there will be no room for negotiating or eliminating these expenses. On the other hand, some of your other expenses may not be so immediate, nor be considered "needs," but you may still prefer them when the extra money is available. When you have the whole picture in front of you and see the total cost, it will be easier to make decisions about how to handle those expenses when the money is still tight.

Be sure to review the list of suggested additional non-monthly expenses in Roadmap 2.7, so that you can take full advantage of this yearly budget worksheet and include all the necessary valuable information. In addition, the following sections offer a few notes for some of the categories.

Home/yard maintenance. This can include expenses that range from having your carpets cleaned to an addition to your house or backyard. If you have been thinking about reupholstering your furniture and have been trying to decide when you can afford it, use your yearly budget worksheet for your planning.

Auto expenses. If you stop to think this area through ahead of time, you can estimate when you might need tires or need to take your car in for its 60,000-mile checkup. This would also naturally include oil changes; probably other expenses also.

Medical expenses. These are often difficult to know in advance, yet it is helpful to think about the different areas on the suggestion list (in Roadmap 2.7) ahead of time so that you can *anticipate* a possible expense rather than *react* to it. Put some estimate down, even the small co-pays, to remind you of the expenses throughout the year.

Vacations. Plan your vacations in advance. Keep in mind the mini-weekend trip as well as those holiday family visits and summer vacations. Vacations are good practice places for learning to live within your income. You may enjoy going on exotic vacations, but if this puts a hardship on your budget, you may have to reevaluate your priorities. Either spend less in this category or plan to cut back in other categories.

Gifts. For some households, these are a minimal expense. Yet for others who place a high priority on gifts, it could be a major expense remembering holidays, birthdays (including the party expenses), weddings, baby showers, graduation, etc. Planning out all this information ahead of time will make it all more manageable.

Holiday events. This expense will vary from household to household depending on how you celebrate July 4th, Halloween, Thanksgiving, and other traditional and religious events in your family. Don't forget the cost of decorating your house or attending/hosting parties along with all the other related expenses. By listing these estimates as well as the others on this page, you will have a more realistic approach to all your upcoming expenses.

Summary of Where Your Money Goes Over the Year. All of these various expenses are just more examples of "where the money goes." Once you have taken time to estimate and project your upcoming non-monthly expenses,

Roadmap 2.7

Suggested Additional Non-Monthly (Occasional) Expenses

You can either complete this information here, and then transfer it to your yearly budget worksheet (see Roadmap 2.6), or you can use this as your guideline as you fill in the Roadmap directly from these ideas. Some of the expenses listed may be a monthly expense for you. If so, enter those expenses on your monthly budget worksheet (see Roadmap 2.8), *not here*. The focus of the yearly budget worksheet is only on your periodic, quarterly, semiannual, annual, and non-monthly expenses.

Description	Amount(s)	Months Due
Housing		
Property Taxes		
Homeowners Insurance/Renter's Insurance		
Association/Condo Dues		
Storage/Garage/PO Box		
Yard/Garden Supplies		
Yard Service/Maintenance		
Pool Chemicals/Maintenance		
Pest/Termite Control		
Security System		
Home Improvement Projects		
Home Repairs/Maintenance		
Carpet Cleaning/Window Cleaning		
Dry Cleaning (drapes, bedding)		
Home Furnishings/Decorating		
Furniture/Appliances/Electronic Equipment		
Maintenance Agreements		
Other _____		

Utilities (Non-Monthly)										
Fuel/Propane										
Firewood										
Waste Management										
Water/Water Softener										
Other _____										

Transportation										
Vehicle #1 Insurance										
Vehicle #2 Insurance										
Boat/RV/Motorcycle Insurance & Expenses										
Emission Inspection										
License Renewal/Registration										
Oil Change/Tune-up										
Other Maintenance and Repairs										
Other _____										

Health										
Other Insurance										
Medical Exams/Lab Tests										
Visits (sick kids, allergy, etc.)										
Physical Exam/School Physical										
Prescriptions										
Chiropractor										
Dermatologist										
Dental Exams/X-rays/Cleanings										
Dental Work Needed										
Orthodontia										
Vision Exam/Glasses/Contacts										
Alternative Health Practitioners										
Vitamins/Supplements/Homeopathic										
Other _____										

Roadmap 2.7 (continued)

Insurance (Other)	Life Insurance		
	Disability Insurance/Long-Term Care		
	Other _____		
Memberships	Church/Temple		
	Country Club		
	Credit Card Annual Fees		
	Gym Annual Fees		
	Organizations/Clubs		
	Professional Dues/License		
	Auto Club		
	Sports		
	Warehouse Clubs		
	Other _____		
Computer	Hardware/Software		
	Upgrades/Printer Supplies		
	Service/Maintenance		
	Classes/Training/Assistance		
Education (Adult)	Tuition		
	Book/Supply Expenses		
	Trade Journals/Magazines/Newspapers		
	Workshops/Seminars/Speakers		
	Other _____		
Clothing (Adults and Children)	Work Clothes/Uniforms/Shoes		
	Seasonal Clothes/Shoes/Jackets		
	Sports Clothes/Special Events		
	Dry Cleaning/Alterations/Shoe Repair		

Recreation (Adults)	Parties		
	Concerts/Sports Events/Season Tickets		
	Fees: Permits/Tournament/League		
	Hobbies/Sports Equipment and Maintenance		
	Lessons		
	Other ____		
Vacation/ Trips	Transportation		
	Lodging/Meals/Snacks		
	Sights/Activities/Theatre/Galleries		
	Shopping/Souvenirs/Film & Processing		
Children	Tuition/College Expenses		
	School Supplies		
	Photos/Yearbooks/Class Ring/Letter Jacket		
	Prom/Homecoming (flowers, hair, dinner, etc.)		
	Field Trips/Contests/Expos/Fund-Raising		
	Camp Registration/Supplies		
	Sports Equipment/Fees/Clinics		
	Music Lessons/Equipment/Recitals/Costumes		
	Other ____		
Pets	Pet Food		
	Grooming/Pet Hotel		
	Vet Expense/Shots/Rx/Dental		
	Training/License		
Misc.	Donations/Contributions		
	Tax Preparation		
	Taxes Due/Estimated Taxes		
	Retirement Savings (IRA)		

you have valuable information that shows you which months will be light and which ones will be difficult to deal with. Then, you can evaluate each expense and consider your choices: Can you cut back, postpone, modify, or eliminate an expense? When you total all of these expenses, you will quickly see why it may seem that there is never enough money.

This is where a reserve savings account can help: simply total these expenses and divide by 12 (to get your monthly average), and you can see how much money must be put aside each month to prepare for these upcoming expenses. You then can transfer this amount onto the monthly budget worksheet and list it as reserve savings to help you plan ahead for the month. As you look at this completed Roadmap, what does it tell you?

▶ First, as mentioned above, you can see which months are going to be financially stressful and which ones would be easily managed. Now you have a guideline to let you know which month would be better for taking on additional expenses.

▶ Second, you can see what you ideally need to put aside each month to save for all these expenses. If that amount is too much at this time, pick some of the fixed and most expensive categories, like property tax, gifts, auto repairs, etc., and start putting aside one-twelfth of those totals.

▶ Third, and most significant, that monthly average amount is how much you are "affected" indirectly each month by these expenses. This effect or impact usually shows up in the form of added credit card debt, more or larger loans, financial juggling, doing without, and overall frustration.

Now that you can see this, it will help you understand your overall budget each year, and determine if you need to do something about it. This Roadmap is your guideline and is meant to be as flexible as possible. You are the one who decides how to utilize the Roadmap and the information to your best advantage.

▶ Planning Mile by Mile: Create a Monthly Budget

The *monthly budget worksheet* (shown in Roadmap 2.8) is your next critical tool. As you begin each new month, use this Roadmap to streamline your whole bill-paying and budget-planning process. This form helps you to anticipate all your bills as well as the majority of your incidental expenses (getting a haircut, your son's field trip, photo developing, etc.) so you know and can project ahead of time (before the month even begins) how much money you will need for the entire month. You will immediately see if you are going to be short so you have the time to start making some arrangements and changes. You also will know what you can and cannot afford in terms of impulsive splurge events.

The monthly budget worksheet is designed to provide a guideline for coordinating your monthly bills and expenses with your *take-home* pay. Your monthly bills are often easier to remember because most bills come in the mail. Forgotten, however, are the expenses such as meals eaten out, haircuts, gifts, books, tapes, seminars, and the like that often throw off the monthly budget.

The monthly budget worksheet is especially helpful during those lean times when your work hours may be reduced and the amount of bills to pay exceeds the money coming in. This guideline will give you a better overall picture of your monthly obligations and lifestyle expenses. The categories are kept general to allow for flexibility and necessary additions based on your own personal financial needs. Often something as simple as this Roadmap can be the difference between financial chaos and financial control. And chaos is the last thing you need in your life right now.

To use the monthly budget worksheet (Roadmap 2.8), start with the top row next to Income Source and indicate in each column where your money is coming from for that month, whether it is from your job, your checkbook balance rolled over from the previous month, investment or rental income, savings, a refund, etc.

Next, on the second row next to Net Income Total Amount near the top in each column, write down the *net amount* of each paycheck or other money that you will use to pay for those monthly expenses. How many columns you fill in depends on how often you are paid each month. Of course, there are many job situations where the amount may vary or is not always known, such as with commission sales. If this is the case, make a very *conservative* estimate until the actual amount is known.

Notice the emphasis on *net* income and not on *gross* income. This way you are dealing only with the cash you actually have for paying your bills.

On the third row under the Income Source amount, there is room to add the date you receive each paycheck. This will help with your planning when working around due dates and paying your bills.

Roadmap 2.8

Monthly Budget Worksheet

INCOME SOURCE:

Net Income Total Amount:

Expenses	Amount	Date Due	Date Paid	Date Rcv.:							
Fixed Amounts											
Mortgage/Rent											
Car Payments											
Other Loans											
Internet Access											
Insurance											
Clubs/Dues											
Savings											
Fixed Variable											
Electricity											
Oil/Gas											
Water/Garbage											
Telephone/Cell Phone											
Cable TV/Satellite											

Fixed Variable	Groceries										
	Meals Out										
	Auto Expense/Gas										
	Church/Charity										
Occasional	Household										
	Personal										
	Clothes										
	Medical										
	Child Expense										
	Recreation										
	Miscellaneous/Mad Money										
Installment	Credit Cards										
Total	Total Income										
	Total Expense										
	Total Excess										
	Total Short										

Finally, total all of the income and other sources of money across the top row and enter that total amount in the box at the bottom left corner of the page right next to Total Income.

Now let's look at all those bills. In the second column called Amount, list every bill and expense you are expecting that particular month. The bills would be obvious ones, but don't forget about the incidental bills like planning to buy a new suit, attending a workshop, or having your computer serviced that month. This is not necessarily an *average* monthly budget that is being developed, but it could turn out to be one. The real purpose here is to keep track of the unique expenses in the coming month. For example, if your relatives are coming to visit for a week next month, your grocery, meals out, utility, gasoline, and entertainment amounts will all go up. These are unique expenses for that month.

This *proactive planning* budgeting approach is better than the standard method of taking the total of annual expenses and dividing it by 12 months for a monthly average. You can also use this Roadmap to learn how to coordinate the timing of your income with the due dates and needs of your expenses. Many people finally understand how to manage their finances when they learn how to work the payments and general expenses according to the timing of the income. Once they learn this unique art, they will no longer pay all their bills with the first paycheck and then figure out how to live the next week with no money until the paycheck comes.

Other people use this Roadmap to plan how much cash to pull out each week for various cash expenses. By doing this they eliminate all the unnecessary runs to the ATM machine. This Roadmap will definitely help you become *proactive* and more relaxed in your approach to managing money instead of staying in a *reactive* mode. So now let's review how to fill in the expenses in the Amount column.

Pay Yourself First. Notice that Miscellaneous Spending/Mad Money and Savings are under Fixed Amounts on Roadmap 2.8. You've probably heard the phrase "pay yourself first" many times. It is a valid statement because if you penny-pinch to the point where there is no money left for Miscellaneous Spending/Mad Money, you will end up frustrated and disappointed with the whole budget idea. And you certainly don't need any more pain in your life right now. Miscellaneous Spending/Mad Money should be yours to do with as you please. Decide how much Miscellaneous Spending/Mad Money each member of your family needs to allow for little splurges and yet not ignore the necessary expenses.

Just as important under Fixed Amounts is Savings. Again, this is paying yourself first. Consider your savings as an *obligation,* setting aside a specific amount or percentage of your check at the same time you are completing the other categories of the Roadmap. In this manner, you will be thinking of savings as an expense, so that it is planned for regularly and not dependent on leftover funds.

You should have different savings accounts—*reserve* (for upcoming known bills and expenses listed on your yearly budget worksheet [refer back to Roadmap 2.6]), *emergency* (equivalent to three months of take-home pay for unknown disasters), and *goals* (a wish list)—and try to save regularly for them.

Once you have saved enough money for your reserve and emergency accounts, you will realize that it is actually possible to save money. Saving for your goals soon becomes more exciting and challenging as you realize that it is now possible to reach your goals.

Test Drive Your Budget: Estimating Some of Your Monthly Expenses

In many cases, such as your utilities bills or other areas under Fixed Variable and Occasional on your monthly budget (again, see Roadmap 2.8), the exact amount of a bill is unknown. For those categories, this is where your budgeting practice comes in: You'll need to estimate the bills until you find out the exact amount.

Remember also to keep in mind those other expenses that are not seen as bills but show up on a daily basis: groceries, gas, entertainment, clothing, etc. You need to plan for these as well. Here you will take an estimated guess (budget) as to what you will need and the amount you can spend. Use a monthly expense record for tracking your expenses each month (see Roadmap 2.10), so that when estimating you'll have a better sense of some averages to use for these categories. Once you become familiar with estimating your expenditures, you will successfully begin to live within your new budget. If your budget is realistic, you will soon choose to eliminate certain unnecessary items to remain within your projected budget.

Your regular monthly household expenses and your actual monthly spending are the final and most important tools that let you know where all your money went that month. This is your reality check on what your spending habits (like the coffee and bagel, CDs, and books, etc.) are actually costing you. Roadmaps 2.9 and 2.10 can help you get a handle on these.

Roadmap 2.9

Basic Monthly Household and Personal Expenses

Expense	Jan.	Feb.	Mar.	Apr.	May	June
Estimated Taxes						
Fixed: Mortgage/Rent						
Car Payment/Lease						
Loans						
Insurance						
Variable: Utilities						
Phones						

Groceries												
Gasoline												
Credit Cards:												
Major Periodic Expenses:												
TOTAL EXPENSES												
Total Income (page 63)												
Difference												
Deposit into Savings*												
Withdraw from Savings												

Before you total your Amount column in Roadmap 2.8, think again if there is anything else that may be coming up as an expense for the particular month you are outlining. Look at the categories on the monthly expense record (in Roadmap 2.10) and the list of common expenses (in Roadmap 2.7) and see if they trigger any ideas for possible expenses. And finally, look again at your yearly budget worksheet (Roadmap 2.6). If you have not put the 1/12th into reserve savings, did you include those unique expenses when planning for this particular month?

Now it's time to tally up and face your total. Put that total figure for this column Amount at the bottom next to Total Expenses in Roadmap 2.8. As you filled in this column, you probably were already telling yourself this is more than you have coming in. If that is the case, now that you can see it in black and white you'll know why you feel the financial crunch and why those expenses probably ended up on your credit cards.

Remember, *this Roadmap needs to be done before the month begins.* It is a projection of your anticipated budget. That means you now have the time and opportunity to take charge and do something about this information. You always have the following choices: postpone, cut back, eliminate, or bring in more income.

What can you eliminate? For starters, there are the lattes, books, CDs, meals out, full-price movies, clothes, and gadgets. Ask yourself, do you *really need* them? Likely not! Reevaluate each expense.

What else can you do? How can you bring more money in? Can you get more overtime hours or a part-time job? Do you have enough stuff to have a yard sale? What if you took your used books, CDs, and clothes to the resale shops for some extra cash?

In the meantime, you have been probably building a small emergency fund and can cover expenses this time by withdrawing the necessary amount. But don't make this a habit. Touch your emergency fund only as an absolute last resort. It is very important to replenish the fund by planning your cutbacks for the next few months.

▶ Scheduling Your Pit Stops: Timing Your Income to Your Payments and Expenses

Now that you have reworked your numbers so that your expenses match your income, go back to the top of the Amount column in the Fixed Amounts section of your monthly budget worksheet in Roadmap 2.8. Based on due dates and income dates, distribute and balance the more expensive bills over the different pay periods in each column. If some pay periods, like the beginning of the month, are pretty top-heavy with bills, try contacting those creditors and figure out if you can time your future payment date with your paycheck dates.

Another method is to allocate small portions from some or all of the paychecks to cover a large bill, such as your mortgage. You don't write one big check, you write small checks for that *big* amount. This is what you can do—itemize a portion under different pay periods, keep a record of that amount or actually go ahead and write a check for it and keep it in the envelope until the final check and full amount is ready. Then send the envelope with the multiple checks totaling the complete payment.

Categories like groceries, gasoline, and eating out are generally divided somewhat under each pay period. You decide how best to balance all the expenses under each of the Income columns. Keep working with a pencil, as it may take some fine-tuning to balance each of the Income columns with the expenses.

▶ Don't Rely On Cruise Control: Getting Control of Your Finances

You have just completed an important step in getting and keeping control of your finances. Of course, doing a monthly budget worksheet does not change or increase the amount of actual money you have or will earn. Being aware, however, of where and how your money is being spent will give you the feeling that you are beginning to control your money. It will help you stretch the use of those dollars more than ever before. And this feeling of control will give you some peace of mind at this difficult time in your life.

A final suggestion: Your monthly budget worksheet is actually an *ideal tool* to use if you are ready to simplify your bill-payment process but prefer to continue using a hands-on system for outlining your monthly bills and expenses. Visually, you have everything down on one sheet and can easily see the amounts and dates for each of the bills.

To streamline the process of actually paying all those bills, you have a number of convenient cashless choices. You may already be using automatic bank withdrawals for utilities and loan payments on your home, cars, and

Roadmap 2.10

Monthly Expense Record

Balance Forward from Last Month: Cash _____ Checking _____ Savings _____

NET INCOME

SALARY/COMMISSIONS				TOTAL
TOTAL INCOME				

OTHER				
TOTAL INCOME				

SAVINGS

(Describe)				
TOTAL SAVINGS				

INVESTMENTS/RETIREMENT

TOTAL INVESTMENTS				

FOOD

	groceries	fast food / dining out / school lunches	tobacco / alcohol / snacks / beverages / water
W			
E			
E			

HOUSEHOLD

cleaner / mainten. / house / yard / pool	appliances / furniture / furnishings / supplies	postage / ATM fees / bank chg. / misc.	interest / taxes

TRANSPORTATION

gas	auto / mainten. / wash / license	taxi / transit / tolls / parking

PERSONAL

clothing / alterations / dry clean. / laundry / shoe care	toiletries / cosmetics / hair / nails / massage

HEALTH

doctor / dentist / vision / medicine / vitamins	personal growth / therapy

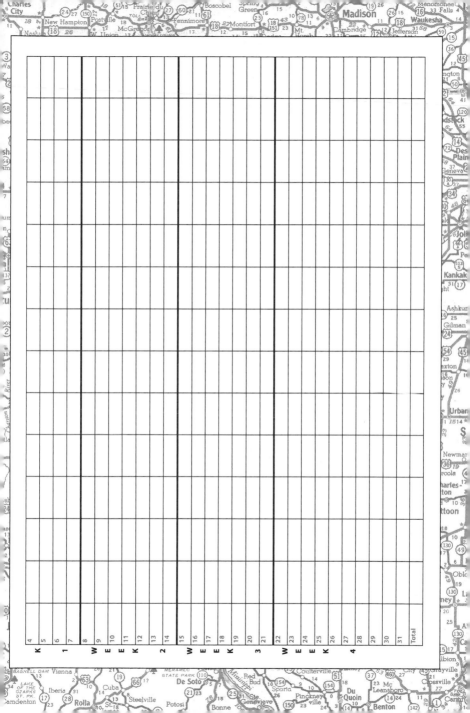

	4	5	6	7	8	9	10	11	12	13	14	15	16	17	18	19	20	21	22	23	24	25	26	27	28	29	30	31	Total
	K	1			W	E	E	K	2			W	E	E	K	3			W	E	E	K	4						

other loans. Many people also choose to use their credit card for automatically paying fixed and regular monthly bills. They then pay the bill in full, enjoying the convenience and other benefits they receive by using a particular credit card.

Often, there are still payments due to small businesses and individuals who will only take checks. This is where online bill payment services through your bank or other service providers come handy. A majority of the services will pay any bill for you. Once you have signed up for the online service, all you have to do is enter the information for your new payee, indicate which account to use, how much to pay and when, and you are done. (Refer back to Chapter 1 and to Appendix B for more information on online bill-paying services.)

If you aren't quite ready to start paying your bills online, you should still know that your bank probably offers online banking. This means you can check your current balance and see what checks have cleared at any time as you work out your plan with the monthly budget worksheet. This may be the perfect way for you to slowly transition to online financial services that can ease a lot of your burden. This will help you focus on more important things in your life right now.

Plan Your Trip

Develop a Long-Term Financial Plan

Once you've assessed your current financial situation and completed your basic budget for the short term, you should begin to think about your longer-term financial plans. We introduced some of this in Chapter 1, where we suggested that you "take on passengers" for this part of your life's journey, because you'll need help from qualified professionals in various areas. This chapter focuses on getting help from a financial planner to orchestrate your plans, an attorney to update (or create) your will and estate plans; and an accountant to help with tax planning and other considerations. Let's get started.

▶ Long-term Travel Plans: Update Your Will and Estate Plans

Once you have lost your spouse, the estate plan the two of you created should kick into action. That's assuming you have done some estate planning. If you didn't, it will be more difficult to reestablish your financial foundation after your spouse's death. But don't despair; this chapter will help you through this, too.

However, if you're reading this book when your spouse is terminally ill, you still have time to write a will and set up trusts. The will should spell out whom you wish to care for minor children, how your assets are to be distributed, and who will serve as executor of your estate. Working with a knowledgeable estate-planning attorney, divide your assets between yourself and your spouse to minimize estate taxes. Married couples can transfer any amount of assets to their surviving spouse. However, each individual is limited to $2 million (as of 2006; $3.5 million in 2009) worth of assets to non-spousal beneficiaries free of estate tax.

Check Your Mirrors: Recognize the Importance of Your Will and Estate Plans

If your spouse has passed away, it's even more important for you to write or update your own will—especially if you have children. Being the parent of a minor child—that is, a child younger than 18 or 21, depending on the state in which you live—provides you with a special reason for writing a will. A will provides you with a legal vehicle to designate an adult or adults (married or not) who would raise your child in the event of your death. The designated individual is called a personal guardian. Think carefully about who you are picking for this important job of rearing your child.

Even if you don't have minor children (or any children for that matter), updating your estate plan (or creating one, if you don't already have one) is a very smart thing to do and will help bring you peace of mind. You can feel good about the fact that you have planned ahead to ease the burdens your loved ones will face at your death. If you don't make any estate plan, your family is likely to face legal and financial problems. In many ways, estate planning can be considered the ultimate act of love.

Along with your will you should create a *power of attorney,* which gives someone you trust—like a family member, friend, or lawyer—the right to make important health or financial decisions in the event you become incapacitated. You also should prepare and sign a *living will,* which states your desires about being kept alive through extreme life-saving measures or being allowed to die if you are unable to make those decisions yourself. Keep the will, power of attorney, and living will up-to-date by reviewing it regularly. Some healthcare providers are now requiring that healthcare directives be updated or re-signed and dated every six months.

One of the most common trusts used today is the *living trust,* which allows your heirs to sidestep probate court. While you are alive, you move all your assets into the trust by retitling assets. When you die, those assets pass directly to your heirs as defined within your trust document.

When you hear the word *estate,* you may envision something big and grandiose and far beyond your own financial reality—a mansion, perhaps. However, in the eyes of the law, your estate is simply everything you own, individually or with others. Your home, car, furniture, bank accounts, jewelry, life insurance policy, retirement plan, stocks and bonds, and other assets are all part of your estate. Good estate planning lets you accomplish six key goals:

1. It enables you to name the guardians of your minor children and the custodians of the money to help provide their support.
2. It ensures that when you die, your property will legally transfer to whomever you wish. The people who receive your property are called your beneficiaries.
3. It provides for the orderly processing of creditor claims against your estate. The probate process sets a deadline by which claims must be filed for possible payment. Creditors who do not meet that deadline do not get their claims paid.
4. It minimizes any taxes your estate may owe after you die, leaving more for your beneficiaries. Tax minimization is typically a concern only for people with substantial estates. (This is discussed in more detail in the next section of this chapter.)
5. It plans for the possibility that you may become seriously injured or ill and unable to manage your own finances. Estate planning allows you to legally designate the person you want to manage your finances if you can't.
6. It establishes legal mechanisms to direct your health care when you are unable to make these decisions for yourself and when you are near death with no hope of recovery and unable to make your own decisions. Without the appropriate legal mechanisms, your estate could be depleted by the cost of life-sustaining medical care and treatment you might not want if you could speak for yourself.

Roadmap 3.1 offers more information on how estate planning can help you at this time.

What Estate Planning Can Accomplish

▶ Provide financially for your dependent children and others after you die. *Financial planning* is something you do to build and preserve your wealth and to provide for your well being. *Estate planning* is something you do to help ensure that the assets you accumulate during your lifetime that are not needed for your support go to the people or causes you want them to.

▶ Arrange for the care and financial well-being of your young children should you die while they are still minors. Depending on your state, a minor is a child who is either under 18 or 21 years of age.

▶ Legally transfer your property to your beneficiaries.

▶ Control, even after your death, the access your beneficiaries have to the money and other assets you leave them.

▶ Ensure that the maximum amount of your estate goes to your beneficiaries rather than toward paying probate costs, legal and executor fees, and other expenses.

▶ Minimize the inheritance taxes your estate may be liable to pay and arrange for the payment of any taxes that may be due. Estate taxes are a concern only for those of you who have substantial estates.

▶ Minimize any delays in the distribution of the assets in your estate to your beneficiaries.

▶ Minimize potential creditor claims against your estate when you die and fund the debts your estate must pay.

▶ Plan for the future of your business should you become physically or mentally incapacitated, or in the event of your death.

▶ Arrange for the management of your finances and medical care should you become so seriously injured or ill that you cannot manage your own affairs.

▶ Plan and fund your funeral and burial or cremation.

Writing a will is not just something that rich people or older people should do. Anyone who has assets or minor children should prepare one. Depending on your situation, a will may be the only estate planning tool you need to use; however, if you use other tools—you set up a living trust, for example —you still need an up-to-date and legally valid will.

If You Have a Minor Child and Do Not Write a Will. In many states, a will is the *only* legal vehicle you can use to name a personal guardian for your minor child. Therefore, if you die without having named a personal guardian for your child, the court will decide who will assume that responsibility. Bottom line: The person who ends up raising your child may be the person you would have named or it could be someone you do not like, respect, or even know.

If an adult relative cares for your young child without the legal designation of personal guardian, problems will arise because the adult would not have a legal right to make decisions for your child. For example, your child might not be eligible for the guardian's medical insurance plan, register your child for school, or give the consent for your child to receive certain kinds of medical care. To get those and other legal rights, your child's unofficial guardian would have to initiate a court process to be named legal guardian.

Every state limits the total value of the assets a minor can own without having an adult to manage them on the child's behalf. If you write a will, you can designate that responsibility to the adult, or property guardian. However, if you die without having written a will and the value of the assets your child inherits exceeds your state's maximum, the court will appoint a property guardian. This person will manage your child's inheritance until your child becomes a legal adult.

The adult the court appoints may be a relative, a close friend, or a professional property guardian. That person may be the same individual appointed by the court to serve as your young child's personal guardian if you didn't have a will. If a professional is appointed, your child's estate will have to pay an annual fee as long as the person serves as a property guardian. If a relative or friend is appointed, the person might not necessarily be a good money manager or someone you would want to entrust with that job.

You should also designate in your will an alternate personal guardian just in case your first choice were unable or unwilling to carry out that responsibility. If you want you can also name two people as coguardians for your minor child. This arrangement may make sense if the coguardians are married or in a committed, unmarried relationship. (However, keep in mind that, in a society where an estimated 50 percent of all marriages fail, you may be creating potential problems down the road if the coguardians divorce or the coguardians' unmarried partnership ends.)

After your death, a court must confirm the appointment of your child's guardian, a process that is usually completed without a hitch unless someone comes forward to contest the appointment. If there are problems, a hearing will be held to determine what is in the best interest of your child.

If You Have Children from a Prior Relationship. If you are divorced and have custody of your child from that marriage, when you die, by law, your ex-spouse would ordinarily get full legal responsibility for the child unless deemed legally unfit to parent.

If you would prefer that your ex-spouse not raise your child, you can say so in your will and name the person you prefer to have that responsibility. However, because your reasons for making this request are probably not flattering to your ex, it's usually not a good idea to state them in your will. If you do, your ex-spouse may sue your estate for libel because your will becomes part of the public record through the probate process. It may be better to provide your executor with a written statement of your reasons for asking that your ex-spouse not raise the child. If you have any records or other documents that support your request, attach copies of them to the statement. Also, if you have the resources, leave money in your will for your executor or one of your beneficiaries to pursue a contest of guardianship should the situation arise. If you anticipate this could be the case, be sure to talk with your attorney, executor, and desired guardian to explain why you want the contest.

Despite what your will says, the truth is that a judge would probably award child custody to your ex-spouse unless your ex-spouse does not want that responsibility or the court deems that the person is an unfit parent. Ongoing problems with drugs or alcohol, a criminal record, a history of serious mental illness, a failure to be actively involved in your child's life for a long time, among other things, could induce a judge to make that determination.

Qualities to Look for When Choosing a Personal Guardian. It goes without saying that the person you choose as personal guardian for your child should be someone of good character who shares your basic values. More important, the person should be willing to respect any special wishes you may have regarding how you want your child brought up. For example, you may want your child to be raised in a specific religion, or perhaps you do not want your child to receive any religious education at all. Obviously, your child's personal guardian should not have a drug or alcohol problem or a history of emotional problems. Most important, however, that person should have the time for and the interest in taking on the role of guardian.

Many grandparents end up raising their grandchildren because the children's parents did not write a will or did not designate a personal guardian for their kids in their wills. However, a grandparent may be elderly and is more apt to become seriously ill or to die while a child is still a minor. He or she may not have the energy and stamina necessary to raise a young and active child. As compared with a younger adult, they might also find it tougher to cope with issues like drugs, sexuality, violence, and so on.

Broach this topic if your child is old enough to have opinions about who should be the guardian, but be sensitive about it — the conversation would be emotionally upsetting for your child at any time, but especially at this time. Listen carefully if your child raises serious objections to a potential guardian.

Consequences of Dying Without a Will. Understanding what can happen if you die without a will, or *intestate,* helps underscore why you need one. After you die, nothing may happen at first. No official will knock at your family's door or send them a letter about the problems and expenses your family may face because you died without a will. However, your family may begin fighting with one another about who should get the assets you own, especially if your estate is substantial or if bad blood already exists within your family. Although that sort of conflict is possible even with a will, having one helps minimize that potential.

Another result of not writing a will is that your estate will probably incur fees and expenses it wouldn't otherwise. Those fees and expenses will be paid by your estate, leaving less of it for your family members or other beneficiaries.

That's not all; there are other consequences of not writing a will. First, a probate judge will appoint an administrator to perform the duties your executor would have performed had you named one in your will. That person may or may not be someone your family knows or trusts. Also, the administrator will be entitled to receive a fee from your estate for the services, which further reduces the assets that you want to distribute to the people and causes of your choice.

Second, the probate judge, not you, will decide who inherits the assets in your estate based on the inheritance laws of your state. Those individuals are your legal heirs but they might not be the ones you would want to end up with your assets. Typically, for widows and widowers, your children are first in line to inherit your assets, followed by your parents, siblings, nieces and nephews, and so on. The exact distribution pattern depends on the laws of your state. If you have no surviving relatives, your property goes to the state.

Other possible consequences of having a court determine who gets what include:

▶ Each of your children would probably receive the same share of your estate even though their respective financial circumstances might be very different.

▶ Relatives you don't like or maybe don't even know could inherit from your estate.

▶ The court will give nothing to your special friends or favorite charity. According to the terms of the law, the judge is legally bound to distribute your assets to your legal heirs (next of kin).

▶ Don't Travel Solo: Get Help from an Estate Lawyer

Theoretically, if your estate is relatively modest, if your family situation is not complex—that is, you don't have children from multiple marriages, everyone in your family gets along with one another, for example—and if your estate planning goals are simple and straightforward, you can prepare your own simple will.

Still, it's best to hire an attorney to write a will for you. Roadmap 3.2 outlines numerous reasons why hiring an attorney's help is advisable. Perhaps the most important reason is that an attorney can help you ensure that your will meets the current legal requirements of your state and will stand up in court after you die. If you write a will that is not legally valid, it will not be recognized by the probate court and it amounts to not writing a will at all.

Procrastination is another excellent reason to hire a lawyer to handle your will, especially at this difficult time. Let's be honest: If you're like most people, the last thing you want to do right now is write your will. Hiring a lawyer means that the task will be accomplished.

Roadmap 3.2

Eight Good Reasons for Hiring an Attorney to Help Write Your Will

1. It's easy to put off writing your own will. Hiring an attorney means you'll actually have a will.
2. An attorney will not charge you a fortune to draft a simple will, which is the type of will most people need.
3. With an attorney's assistance, you don't run the risk of preparing a will that won't stand up in court or that won't accomplish your estate planning objectives.
4. An attorney can identify potential problems related to your estate, as well as the solutions to those problems.
5. An attorney can tell you if you should combine a will with other estate planning tools.
6. If you are a business owner, an attorney can tell you about the special estate planning issues you face and how to address them. Those issues include business succession and liquidity.
7. An attorney can explain how the probate process works and help you prepare for it. Probate is a legal process that affects the transfer of the property in your will to your designated beneficiaries, among other things.
8. If estate taxes are a concern for you, an attorney can help you minimize the amount of taxes your estate will be liable for.

An additional benefit of working with a lawyer is the estate planning advice and information you would never have access to if you wrote your own will. For example, a lawyer should be able to help save your estate money on professional fees, taxes, and court costs, among other things. The lawyer can also point out other estate planning tools you should use in addition to a will; and if you are concerned that there may be costly contests to your will after you die, the lawyer can help you plan ahead for how to deal with them.

An attorney's help won't cost you a lot—probably between $500 and $1,500 depending on how complex your estate planning issues are. Many estate attorneys will provide you with a will that includes a testamentary trust (i.e., a trust that is part of your will and not funded until after you die) as well as a durable power of attorney and a living will for $1,000 or less. The exact amount you pay depends, among other things, on where you live (attorneys in large metropolitan areas tend to charge more than attorneys in rural areas), the complexity of your estate, the types of assets you own, and whether you are concerned that your will may be contested or that there may be creditor problems after you die.

Even if your estate is small, don't assume that you can do without an attorney. Bad idea! In fact, it can be argued that you need an attorney's help more than someone with a substantial estate. Consider this: If your estate is worth $900,000, and you make a mistake that costs your estate $10,000, that would reduce your estate by only 1 percent, but if your estate is worth $90,000 and you make that same mistake, your estate will be reduced by 11 percent, a much more significant amount to your heirs.

To locate a qualified estate planning attorney in your area, get a reference from a friend, a family member, your CPA, or financial advisor; contact your local or state bar; or go to the Web site of the American College of Trust and Estate Counsel and Martindale-Hubbard (see Appendix B for details).

What Constitutes a Substantial Estate? You don't need to worry about minimizing the amount of federal estate taxes your estate will have to pay after your death unless your estate is substantial. The definition of a *substantial estate* has changed over the years, but in 2006 it is defined as an estate that is worth more than $2 million and in 2009, it will rise to $3.5 million. In 2010, the estate tax will be eliminated, for one year only, and then the following year reinstated at $1 million. However, depending on the political climate in the coming years, Congress could repeal or modify these changes. It is important, therefore, to stay in touch with your estate planning attorney.

For some people, a car, furniture, and your household and personal items may represent your entire estate. Most likely, their total value does not come close to the threshold for federal estate tax liability. However, if you are a homeowner, have adequate life insurance, and have accumulated other assets like retirement benefits and stocks and bonds, you may be surprised to discover that unless you do the appropriate planning, when you die, your estate will have to pay federal estate taxes. Depending on your state, your estate may be liable for state estate taxes too. For all of these reasons, consider hiring an estate planning lawyer to help you prevent unwanted scenarios.

You and your attorney should meet at least once so that the attorney can begin gathering the information needed to write your will. In addition to

What to Pack

Information Your Lawyer Will Need to Write Your Will

- ▶ Amounts and sources of all your income
- ▶ Amounts and sources of all your debts
- ▶ List of all the significant assets you own, their approximate value, and how you own them (joint or separate property, for example)*
- ▶ The deeds and titles to or other ownership paperwork for all the assets you own yourself or have an interest in
- ▶ Current statements for any retirement, pension, IRA, or other employee benefits programs you participate in
- ▶ Life insurance policies—individual and group
- ▶ Current reports for any brokerage and bank accounts that may be in your name alone or that you held jointly with another person*
- ▶ Copies of all trusts you are a grantor for or a beneficiary of
- ▶ Divorce decrees, property settlement agreements, and prenuptial and postnuptial agreements that you and/or your late spouse may be parties to
- ▶ Any wills you may already have
- ▶ Any trusts you may have set up already
- ▶ Names, addresses, and birth dates of your children and other beneficiaries
- ▶ Name and address of the person you designate as your executor
- ▶ If you own a small or closely held business or have an interest in one, your attorney will also want the following information, where applicable:
  1. Partnership agreement
  2. Articles of incorporation
  3. Shareholders' agreement
  4. Limited liability company operation agreement
  5. Corporate bylaws
  6. Business tax returns
  7. Buy-sell agreements

*This provides an opportunity to make certain that all of the retitling of your assets required as a result of the death of your spouse has been done or is now accomplished.

finding out about your estate planning goals and concerns, your attorney will want to find out about your assets as well as your debts and your family situation. "What to Pack" provides a more complete list of information your attorney will likely ask you to provide.

▶ Taking Over the Wheel: Selecting the Executor of Your Will

Your executor is the person you name in your will to act as legal representative of your estate after you die. In all likelihood, you are the executor of your late spouse's estate (most people name their spouse as executor). Your executor works with the probate court to carry out a minimum of five key tasks for your estate:

1. Locate your will
2. Inventory and value your assets
3. Pay all legitimate claims against your estate
4. Pay any taxes your estate may owe
5. Distribute your assets to your beneficiaries

For example, an older child, another family member, or a close friend may make a good executor. Before you name anyone as your executor, however, make sure that your choice for the job is willing to accept it and capable of handling the responsibility, particularly if your estate is complex and quite valuable or if you are concerned that there may be problems after your death that could complicate the probate process. Don't forget to name a substitute or an alternate executor in your will. This person assumes executor duties should your first choice be unable or unwilling to act as executor after you die.

Your executor is legally entitled to be paid a fee for acting as your legal representative, which will be paid by your estate. However, you can stipulate in your will that you don't want your executor to receive a fee. Before you do that talk it over with the person you want as your executor, the person might not want to take on the job unless compensated for it. On the other hand, if you and your executor are especially close, your executor may waive the fee.

If your state requires that your executor be bonded, you can waive that requirement in your will. If you do, there will be more money in your estate to go to your beneficiaries. However, some states require a cash bond if your executor lives out of state.

Hiring a Professional Executor. Rather than designating a friend or relative as your executor, you may prefer to hire a professional executor for your estate. Banks and attorneys most often fill that role. However, professional executors charge a substantial amount of money for their services—money that will come out of your estate. Therefore, using a professional executor makes the most sense in the following situations:

► if your estate is large and complex;
► if you are concerned that your will may be contested; or
► if you have reason to believe that the terms of your will may trigger conflict among your family members; or
► if there is no one in your life who you feel is willing or capable of handling the job.

Appointing Coexecutors. It sometimes makes sense to appoint coexecutors for your will rather than a single executor. For example, if your estate is especially large and complex, you may not want all of the responsibilities of executor to fall on the shoulders of just one person. Another circumstance when a coexecutor arrangement may make sense is when your first choice for executor doesn't live close to you. If you pick a coexecutor who lives nearby, that person can help the other executor with the day-to-day details of administering your estate. Be aware, however, that a coexecutor arrangement can make matters much more complicated if the coexecutors do not work well together. Their interpersonal problems could slow down the probate process.

Some experts suggest that if you choose a professional executor, you name a family member or close friend as coexecutor. The rationale for this suggestion is that having someone work with the professional executor who is attuned to the needs and interests of your family can make the probate process easier on your loved ones.

What to Look for in an Executor. Your executor is responsible for carrying out many important responsibilities on behalf of your estate. Therefore, the person you choose as executor should be conscientious, well organized, fairminded, and not easily intimidated by lawyers, legal documents, paperwork, or court bureaucracies. It is also a good idea if your executor is trusted and respected by your family and has the time to do the job. By the way, your choice for executor must be a legal adult and a U.S. citizen and cannot be a convicted felon.

As mentioned briefly, there is one additional and very important quality you should look for in an executor—a willingness to do the job. An executor's responsibilities are too important to entrust to someone who does not really want to do it. Therefore, it is a good idea to review those responsibilities with your choice for executor so that you can be certain that the person is willing and able to assume them.

After you die, the court must formally approve your executor. Although it rarely happens, the court will appoint someone else to be the executor of your estate if it denies approval of the person you chose.

Duties of an Executor. If you have not done so on behalf of your spouse's estate or as a refresher, the following list describes an executor's typical responsibilities:

- ► Find and review your will
- ► Initiate the probate process with the probate court
- ► Notify all interested parties of your death and of the terms of your will
- ► Identify the assets in your estate that will go through probate and value each of them
- ► Manage the assets in your estate while the probate process is ongoing, which may include paying bills, depositing money, overseeing investments, selling assets, and so on
- ► Pay the legitimate claims of your creditors as well as any taxes your estate may owe
- ► Comply with the reporting requirements of the probate court, file the appropriate legal paperwork, and, as appropriate, notify the Social Security Administration, civil service, Department of Veterans Affairs, and others of your death
- ► Help defend your estate against any contests to your will, albeit most wills are not contested
- ► Communicate with the beneficiaries of your estate about the progress of the probate process
- ► Make sure that your assets are distributed to your beneficiaries according to the wishes you expressed in your will
- ► Prepare a final report for the probate court and formally request that the probate process for your estate be ended

Before you write your will, understand the specific powers your state gives to executors as well as any restrictions your state may impose on them. If you want, you may use your will to give your executor additional powers as appropriate, assuming those other powers do not violate your state's laws. Among other things, those additional powers might include the right to make real estate transactions on behalf of your estate and the right to borrow money to pay your estate's debts.

Most executors hire an estate attorney to help them through the probate process. You may also want to suggest a particular lawyer or law firm if you have a preference. However, you cannot require that your executor follow your wishes regarding legal help. In the end, it is up to your executor whether to hire an attorney and which one to hire.

Depending on the total value of the assets in your probate estate, it may be eligible for a probate process that is less formal, less expensive, and less costly than the traditional probate process, although not every state offers this alternative.

Given the important service that your executor will perform for you and your family, you should do what you can to make your executor's job as easy as possible. The steps you take ahead of time can also help avoid delays in the probate process and save your estate money. Roadmap 3.3 suggests some of the things you can do.

▶ The Road to Riches: Get a Financial Advisor

Once you've taken care of your will and estate plans, consider hiring a financial advisor to help you with all the other new decisions you're facing in your life. In the best of all worlds, the financial planner you hire would be a jack-of-all-financial-trades. The ideal financial planner would be able to do all of the following:

- ▶ know everything about budgeting, investments, taxes, insurance, credit, real estate, employee benefits, estate planning, retirement, college financing, career advancement, and every other aspect of your financial life.
- ▶ help you assess where you stand now, what you want to accomplish, and how you can attain your goals.
- ▶ be personable and a good listener, and maintain objectivity so as not to recommend an investment just because it pays a commission to your financial planner.
- ▶ be your trusted financial advisor.

Do such paragons of virtue exist? Indeed they do, but to find one, you must weed out the incompetent and self-serving neophytes from the professionals.

Roadmap 3.3

What You Can Do Now to Make Your Executor's Job Easier

▶ Be sure your will is legally valid.

▶ Review your will with your executor. Answer your executor's questions and explain the rationale behind any unusual provisions in your will or anything that you believe may upset your family or someone else close to you. Examples of provisions that you should explain include why your will treats your children differently or why you are disinheriting someone in your immediate family.

▶ Let your executor know where you are storing your will. If it is in a home safe or file cabinet, tell your executor where you keep the combination or key.

▶ Give your executor a signed copy of your will.

▶ If you revise your will or revoke it and write a new one, give your executor a copy of the new will.

▶ Explicitly state in your will that you expect your executor to hire professionals as needed to help carry out the duties as executor. This statement will discourage your beneficiaries from complaining if your executor uses the services of an attorney, a CPA, an appraiser, and so on.

▶ Tell your executor where you keep your estate planning worksheet, which lists all your assets and liabilities (you can create this by adapting Roadmaps 2.1 and 2.2, which you created in Chapter 2).

▶ Maintain complete and well-organized records related to your personal finances, property, and investments, and let your executor know where those records are kept. They should include your Social Security number, income tax returns, real estate records, insurance policies, bank accounts, debt documentation, credit card account numbers, records related to your stocks, mutual funds and other investments, ownership papers, and a list of expected death benefits, among other things.

▶ Provide your executor with pertinent information regarding your personal life and family history. This information should include the name of your spouse, a copy of your marriage certificate and your spouse's death certificate, the names of any other spouses as well as copies of any divorce papers, your birth certificate, your naturalization papers, your military records, and the names and addresses of any children, grandchildren, adoptive children, or stepchildren.

- ▶ If you own a business or have an interest in one, make sure your executor knows the location of all pertinent records related to the business and what you want done with your business or business interest after you die. If you want your executor to work with a particular employee, be sure to provide your executor with that person's name, address, and phone number. Also, let that employee know your wishes.
- ▶ Give your executor the names, addresses, and phone numbers of your attorney, financial planner, CPA, banker, insurance agent, stock broker, and any other professional advisors you work with.
- ▶ Write out your desire for your burial or cremation as well as any specific arrangements you have made. Be as detailed as possible. Give your executor a copy.
- ▶ If you have made arrangements to donate any of your organs after you die, put them in writing. Include the name, address, and phone number of the organization/s you want to donate to. Give a copy of this information to your executor.

Before you begin interviewing candidates, though, assess your situation to determine whether you need a financial planner. If you need only one financial service, such as tax return preparation or auto insurance, and know where and how to go about securing those products or services, it is probably not cost effective to pay the fees that a comprehensive financial planner charges, although some planners will charge an hourly or per project fee. On the other hand, if you need an overall strategy that ties together the several aspects of your complex financial picture—past, present, and future—a planner's services may be invaluable. For example, if you have specific long-term goals, such as funding your children's college education or building a retirement nest egg, a financial planner can start you on the right path. You *do* need to think about your future, and feeling confident about your finances will make you feel better in general.

If Your Destination Is a Solid Retirement Plan

If you are a young widow or widower, retirement planning might seem like your least important priority. And, for the short term, it is because you must first adjust both emotionally and financially to a life without your spouse.

However, after this period ends, you should plan seriously for your retirement years. And we've made it easier for you, with some helpful roadmaps.

Tollbooth 3.1 is a worksheet to help you plan what your retirement expenses might be. This can help you estimate how much money you will need to live comfortably in retirement and how much you must save each month to collect enough capital to fulfill that goal. You can use the figures you calculated in Chapter 2 for your income and savings (Roadmap 2.5, the cash flow worksheet includes totals of your income and expenses). Then calculate what you might receive from Social Security in the future, counting both retirement and survivor's benefits. You can obtain these numbers from the Social Security Administration (see Appendix B for contact information).

With this general idea of how much money you will need each year in retirement, examine your potential sources of income. The three main income sources for retirees are Social Security, pensions, and private savings and investments. Based on your earnings and years of service, the Social Security Administration will estimate your benefit in current dollars. Your company's employee benefits department (and your spouse's) can tell you in today's dollars what you should expect to receive from your pension based on your current age and salary level. Adjust both the pension and Social Security figures by the same 4.5 percent inflation factor used in Tollbooth 3.1, your retirement expenses worksheet. To calculate the amount of savings and investments you will need to make up the difference, subtract the adjusted pension and Social Security amounts from your projected annual living expenses.

Finally, to estimate the amount of capital you must amass to generate that level of annual investment income, assuming a 5 percent rate of return, multiply the number by 20. (For example, you need $20,000 in capital to produce $1,000 in interest if it earns 5 percent annually.) If you want to assume a higher rate of return than 5 percent, multiply by a smaller number. For example, multiply by 10 if you want to assume a 10 percent average annual return (because $10,000 will produce $1,000 in interest at 10 percent).

Using the assumptions in Tollbooth 3.1, you would therefore need to amass $312,000 over the next 20 years until retirement if you want to maintain a lifestyle similar to your current lifestyle (see Tollbooth 3.2, which is a capital accumulation worksheet). Of course, many factors can change the amount of capital you need to accumulate. If your pension or Social Security benefit does not rise as fast as inflation, for example, you will require more in

Tollbooth 3.1

Retirement Expenses Worksheet

	Example	Your Situation
1. Present Gross Annual Income	$50,000	$_____
2. Present Annual Savings	$ 5,000	$_____
3. Current Spending (Subtract item 2 from item 1.)	$45,000	$_____
4. Retirement Spending Level (between 80 percent and 100 percent, depending on your lifestyle)	90%	_____%
5. Annual Cost of Living (in Today's Dollars) if You Retire Now (Multiply item 4 by item 3.)	$40,500	$_____
6. 4.5 Percent Inflation Factor (from table below)	2.4	_____
7. Estimated Annual Cost of Living (in Future Dollars) at Retirement (Multiply item 6 by item 5.)	$97,200	$_____

Years until Retirement	Inflation Factor
40	5.8
35	4.7
30	3.7
25	3.0
20	2.4
15	1.9
10	1.6
5	1.2

private savings. However, if you earn a higher return on your investments, you will need to save less. You should also keep in mind that you may live longer and have large health expenses and that there may be changes in Social Security that may affect your benefits.

The next step is to figure out how much money you must save each year before retirement to accumulate the needed capital. The amount of money

Tollbooth 3.2

Capital Accumulation Worksheet

	Example	Your Situation
1. Estimated Annual Cost of Living (in Future Dollars) at Retirement (item 7 from Retirement Expenses Worksheet)	$ 97,200	$_____
2. Annual Pension Income	10,000	_____
3. Inflation Adjusted Pension Income (Multiply item 2 by appropriate inflation factor in Tollbooth 3.1.)	24,000	_____
4. Annual Social Security Benefit	15,000	_____
5. Inflation-Adjusted Social Security Benefit (Multiply item 4 by appropriate inflation factor.)	36,000	_____
6. Inflation-Adjusted Pension and Social Security Income (Add items 3 and 5.)	60,000	_____
7. Amount by Which Expenses Exceed Pension and Social Security Income (Subtract item 6 from item 1.)	37,200	_____
8. Needed Capital (Multiply item 7 by 20.)	$744,000	$_____

you calculated in Item 8 in your capital accumulation worksheet (in Tollbooth 3.2) is not *all* the money you will need to fund your retirement. It is the amount needed to fund *your first year* of retirement. To keep pace with inflation, you must increase your savings by at least 5 percent a year until you reach retirement age. So now let's calculate how much money you must save each year to meet this goal (see Tollbooth 3.3). The sample figures assume an after-tax rate of return of 7.5 percent on all investments and 20 years before retirement, but obviously you should adjust these for your own particular situation.

After running your numbers through the three worksheets, you should have a sense of how much money you need to save and invest each year to meet your retirement savings goal. If you would like to apply different inflation rates, rates of return and change other factors, investigate the software

Tollbooth 3.3

Annual Savings Worksheet

	Example	Your Situation
1. Capital Needed to Fund Retirement (Item 8 from Capital Accumulation Worksheet)	$744,000	$_____
2. Current Investment Assets (Value of Stocks, Bonds, Mutual Funds, and Other Investments)	$30,000	$_____
3. 7.5 percent Appreciation Factor (from table below)	4.2	_____
4. Appreciation of Your Investment Assets until Retirement (Multiply item 2 by item 3.)	$126,000	$_____
5. Other Assets Required by Retirement Age (Subtract item 4 from item 1.)	$618,000	$_____
6. Savings Factor for Years until Retirement (from table below)	.0231	_____
7. Savings Needed over the Next Year (Multiply item 5 by item 6.)	$ 14,276	$_____

Years until Retirement	7.5 percent Appreciation Factor
40	18.0
35	12.6
30	8.8
25	6.1
20	4.2
15	3.0
10	2.1
5	1.4

Years until Retirement	Savings Factor
40	.0044
35	.0065
30	.0097
25	.0147
20	.0231
15	.0383
10	.0707
5	.1722

on the market that is designed to help you calculate how much you need to save for retirement. Appendix B includes a list and descriptions of a few of these.

Saving for Retirement. Next, set up your savings regimen using one of the many *automatic investment programs* offered by mutual funds, banks, stockbrokers, and insurance companies. If your employer gives you the opportunity to contribute to a *tax-deferred retirement plan,* such as a salary reduction 401(k) or profit-sharing plan, take full advantage of the offer. In plans where your employer matches your contributions, invest at least the maximum that is matched. Also, establish a Keogh account if you produce self-employment income, or fund an individual retirement account (IRA) whether or not your contribution is deductible.

If You're Already Retired. If you are widowed while already retired, you confront a different financial situation. If you receive regular income from an annuity, those payments will continue until you die, as long as you and your spouse chose the joint and survivor payout option. However, if your spouse selected the life annuity or term certain option, the annuity payments may stop either right away or within a few years. This is why it is so important to choose an annuity payout option carefully. (Chapter 4 offers more information on insurance.)

Depending on your age, your spouse's earnings record, and whether you have children, you may be eligible for Social Security benefits. You will receive survivor's benefits if you are younger than 60 and support children younger than 16. However, if you are younger than 60 but have no children, you will not yet be eligible to receive survivor Social Security benefits. Nevertheless, register your spouse's death with the Social Security Administration by supplying a copy of your marriage certificate and the death certificate. You will then be eligible for a funeral expense payment of $225.

Widows and widowers between age 60 and 65 are eligible for survivor's benefits from Social Security benefits. However, your monthly check will be less than if you begin receiving benefits at age 65. If your spouse was married to someone else for at least 10 years and then divorced, the former spouse is also entitled to receive Social Security benefits on your spouse's earnings record, as long as the ex-spouse did not remarry. At age 65, you are eligible to sign up for Medicare Part A, which covers hospital charges, and Part B, which reimburses doctors' bills and other nonhospital costs.

If your spouse was an armed forces veteran, you might qualify for an additional pension benefit. You may also be eligible to receive reimbursement of burial and funeral expenses from both federal and state veterans programs, as long as you file a claim within two years of your spouse's death.

Beyond the financial aspects of retirement, you must make many decisions about the kind of lifestyle you want. You may find that the home you shared with your spouse for so many years is too large and expensive to maintain. In that case, you might want to explore continuing-care communities or other housing options. One of the biggest problems for widows and widowers is loneliness, so choose a community in which you can make friends. You also should plan to pursue hobbies, political causes, social activities, educational opportunities, and travel in retirement. Though you may not enjoy participating in these activities as much as you would have with your spouse, make the most of your retirement years.

If Your Destination Is Saving for Your Children's Education

Widows and widowers with children often find the task of financing their children's college education overwhelming. But again, we can help, and let's go slowly. It might seem difficult enough to meet your current expenses on a reduced income, never mind the tens of thousands of dollars that public or private schools cost. You have two solutions to this dilemma: increase your savings, or qualify for more loans. If you are widowed when your children are young, you have enough time to start a college savings plan. The more and earlier you save, the easier it will be to pay tuition bills.

The best way to start is to enroll in an *automatic investment program,* such as one offered by a mutual fund, or in a *payroll deduction savings bond plan.* You may also want to buy shares in a solid company paying a high dividend, such as a utility, and enroll in the *dividend reinvestment plan* (DRIP), which will compound your principal over time effortlessly and at no cost.

You face a different situation if you become widowed when your children are near college age or already enrolled at a university. Without much accumulated savings, you will have to rely on the many grants, loans, and scholarships that are available for financing college. With lower income brought on by your status as a widow or widower, you will likely be considered more in financial need than other families and thereby qualify for more generous grants and loans. Nevertheless, you and your children can be burdened by years of interest payments if you take on too many loans. Apply for as many grants as you can find because grant money need not be repaid.

Finding Your Way: How to Choose a Financial Planner

Once you've determined that you need a financial planner, look into the different professionals who label themselves as such. Anyone can wear the planner tag; no federal, state, or local laws require certain qualifications, such as those imposed on other professionals, including accountants and lawyers. However, several associations and organizations grant credentials that signify a planner's level of education. Some of the most commonly recognized designations follow.

Certified Financial Planner (CFP). This designation is earned by people who have been licensed by the Certified Financial Planner Board of Standards (CFP Board). All licensees have completed financial planning courses through a CFP-Board-registered college or university. These people must complete a 10-hour two-day comprehensive exam to prove their expertise in financial planning, insurance, investing, taxes, retirement planning, employee benefits, estate planning, and risk management. The test is difficult and requires the test taker to apply their financial planning knowledge to three case studies and multiple-choice questions. In addition to having passed the tests, a CFP licensee must possess a certain amount of work experience in the financial services industry, have a defined amount of college education, abide by a strict code of ethics, and fulfill continuing education requirements.

Chartered Financial Analyst (CFA). This designation is earned by those who pass a series of three exams administered by the Association for Investment Management and Research (AIMR) of Charlottesville, Virginia. CFA charter-holders must demonstrate their expertise in investment valuation and management, asset valuation, portfolio management, and industry ethics. CFAs must have a bachelor's degree, adhere to the AIMR Code of Ethics, and have at least three years of work experience and a high level of professional conduct. Many CFAs also have branched out into full-service financial planning. The best time to seek a CFA is when you have a great amount of money to invest and you need the guidance of an investment professional.

Chartered Financial Consultant (ChFC). The ChFC designation is conferred by the American College in Bryn Mawr, Pennsylvania. The ChFC curriculum covers a broad range of financial planning issues. Many ChFCs have particular expertise in life insurance matters. To earn the designation, the financial planner must pass 10 college-level courses on all major topics of personal finance and business planning, possess industry experience, and adhere to strict ethical standards. To maintain the designation, they must obtain continuing education credits.

Personal Financial Specialist (PFS). The PFS is awarded only to people who are already CPAs. To retain their license, they are required to renew their license annually and complete at least 30 hours of continuing education credits every two years. Within the AICPA, those with a PFS concentrate on financial planning. They must be members in good standing of the AICPA, possess at least three years of personal financial planning experience, and demonstrate special expertise by passing a comprehensive financial planning exam. To keep their PFS status, they must be re-accredited every three years, a process that includes continuing education and an extensive peer review.

▶ Ask for Directions: How to Interview a Financial Planner

If you limit your search to financial planners who have earned one or more of these six designations, you will have plenty of qualified planners to choose from. As with any financial professional you consider hiring, arrange a face-to-face interview, where you can get a sense of the planner's personality and areas of expertise.

Following are a few sample questions you should ask prospective financial advisors:

What services do you provide? Most planners will help you assemble a comprehensive plan, whereas others specialize in particular areas of finance. The services you should expect include:

- ▶ cash management and budgeting;
- ▶ education funding;
- ▶ estate planning;
- ▶ investment review and planning;
- ▶ life, health, and property/casualty insurance review;
- ▶ retirement planning;

▶ goal and objective setting; and

▶ tax planning.

Ask about each service specifically.

Will you show me a sample financial plan you have done? Without revealing confidential information or client names, the planner should be glad to show you the kind of plan you can expect when the data-gathering and planning process is complete.

What type of clientele do you serve? Some planners specialize by income category, age, or professional group. For example, if you are nearing retirement, do not hire a planner whose clients are mostly young entrepreneurs. Or if you are a dentist, you might look for a planning firm that specializes in serving dentists or other medical professionals.

Who will I deal with on a day-to-day basis? In larger planning firms, you might see the chief planner only at the beginning and end of the planning process and work with their associates in the meantime. If that is the case, meet the staff with whom you will be working, and ask about their qualifications.

Do you have access to other professionals if my planning process takes us into areas in which you are not an expert? A good planner has a network of top accountants, lawyers, insurance specialists, and investment pros to fall back on.

Do you just give financial advice, or do you also implement the advice on a fee-only basis or by selling financial products? The great fault line in the financial planning industry lies between these two types of professionals.

Will your advice include specific product recommendations, or will you suggest only generic product categories? Most planners will name particular stocks or mutual funds, for example. Others will simply advise that you keep 50 percent of your assets in stocks, 30 percent in bonds, and 20 percent in cash, leaving *you* to determine which stocks, bonds, and cash instruments are appropriate. You should decide how much advice you want from your financial planner.

Will you spend the time to explain your rationale for recommending a specific product and how it suits my goals, my tolerance for risk, and my

circumstances? How do you plan to monitor a recommended mutual fund or investment product once I've bought it?** You should feel comfortable that the planner will make the effort to ensure that you understand the recommended strategy and products as well as their long-term strategy and advice policy.

How will you follow up after you've delivered the plan to ensure that it is implemented? A good planner makes sure that you don't just file away the comprehensive plan and never put it into action. Not only should the plan be implemented, it also should be reviewed and revised as conditions in your life, tax laws, or the investment environment shifts.

How do you get compensated? Some planners charge for the advice they give. Others collect commissions from the sale of products they recommend. And still others charge both a planning fee and a sales charge. (These styles are discussed further in the next section of this chapter.) However your planner gets paid, make sure that you receive a written estimate in advance of the advisor's compensation from all sources and the amount you will be paying directly.

Are there any potential conflicts of interest in the investments you recommend? A planner must inform you, for example, whether the planner's firm earns fees as a general partner in a limited partnership that the planner touts and they must let you know that they receive commissions if they do. Unfortunately, the advisor is not required to disclose how much compensation they receive. However, savvy consumers will ask for the specifics. You must also be informed whether the planner receives some form of payment (commonly known as a *referral fee*) when another firm, such as a law or an accounting firm, is recommended.

Will you have direct access to my money? Some planners want *discretionary control* of their clients' funds, which allows the planners to invest as they see fit. Be extremely careful about agreeing to this arrangement, which is fraught with potential for fraud and malfeasance. If you do agree to it, make sure that the planner is bonded. This insurance will cover you in case the planner runs off with your money. Also, make certain that a reputable third party custodian holds your assets and that you review your statements from this custodian regularly.

What professional licenses and designations have you earned? Besides looking on their walls for diplomas, inquire whether the planner holds a CFA, CFP, ChFC, CPA, or a PFS. Determine whether the planner is licensed to sell securities, which include stocks, bonds, partnerships, and mutual funds. If the planner wants to sell disability, life, and property/casualty insurance, as well as fixed or variable annuities, make sure the planner has a license to sell insurance products. Also find out the planner's educational background. Whether they started out as a lawyer, an insurance agent, an accountant, or some other specialist, it will most likely affect the advice the planner gives.

Is the planner registered as an investment advisor with the Securities and Exchange Commission or your state? All planners who provide investment advice should be registered with either the SEC or your state. If registered, the planner is required to give you Part II of Form ADV or a brochure containing the same disclosure information.

Have you ever been cited by a professional or governmental organization for disciplinary reasons? Even if the planner says there are no blemishes on the record, you can check with the state attorney general's office, the state securities office, and the organizations that grant the professional designation held by the advisor. (Again, see Appendix B.)

Paying the Toll: Find Out How Your Financial Planner Gets Paid

The question of how a financial planner gets paid is a particularly important one as you establish a relationship with your planner. You do not want to be plagued by a nagging fear—especially now, when you have enough on your mind—that your planner recommends products for the commissions they generate rather than for the appropriateness of those products to your situation. In theory, financial planners have an ethical obligation to hold your financial interests above their own, but how they are paid can make that philosophy difficult to execute. Therefore, you should know that planners are compensated in four basic ways, described in the following paragraphs.

Tollbooth Option #1: Commission Only. Such planners offer free consultation and profit only when you buy a product, such as a mutual fund, an annuity, or a life insurance policy. In some cases, the commissions are explicit—for example, a 4 percent front-end load on a mutual fund. In other cases, the fees are lumped into the general expenses of the product, as with life insurance, so you won't know how much your planner makes unless you ask a question about it.

Because a planner who works on commission collects only if you buy, remain aware of their incentives as you consider the planner's advice. When you interview such a planner, ask approximately what percentage of their firm's commission revenue comes from annuities, insurance products, limited partnerships, mutual funds, and stocks and bonds. The planner's answers will give you a sense of the kind of advice their firm usually gives.

Commissions are not only paid up-front, but also as ongoing charges that could apply as long as you hold an investment. For example, mutual funds often levy *12b(1) fees,* which are annual charges of about 1 percent of your assets designed to reward brokers and financial planners for keeping clients in a fund, and insurance companies pay trailing fees to planners for each year a client pays the premiums on an insurance policy.

In other cases, you must pay a fee if you sell a product before a particular amount of time has elapsed. If you want to cash in an annuity or insurance policy early, you must pay surrender charges of 7 percent or so of your investment, part of which reimburses the insurer for the commissions it has paid your planner. If you sell certain mutual funds within four years of buying them, you must remit a *back-end load,* which allows the fund company to recover the up-front sales load it paid your planner. Such back-end loads usually are applied on a sliding scale, so you pay 4 percent if you sell during the first year, 3 percent the second year, 2 percent the third year, and 1 percent the fourth year. After that, you will not be charged a back-end fee.

Many commission-motivated planners also win prizes of merchandise or free travel if their sales of a particular product reach a target level. And *soft-dollar arrangements* award planners with non-cash goods and services, such as computer software, investment research, or magazine subscriptions, if their sales hit certain goals.

You should also ask about sales quotas, or if the advisor in any way is directed to recommend certain financial products over others. Salaries often depend on an advisor's ability to meet sales quotas, and quotas, incentives, and directives can lead to divided loyalties.

Although your planner might not like your questioning their cash payment and other perks, it is your right to know whether the products you buy generate direct income and other benefits for the planner. By knowing the full extent of your planner's compensation, you will be better able to decide whether their advice is objective or self-serving.

Tollbooth Option #2: Fee Only. Some professional planners assess your financial situation for a fee, set in advance, based on time spent with you, a flat dollar amount, or a percentage of your income or assets. Usually, such planners offer a no-cost, no-obligation initial consultation to explore your financial needs. They provide advice on how to implement their recommendations, but they do not collect a dime from commissions if you take their suggestions.

The advantage of this arrangement, of course, is that the planner has no vested interest in having you buy one product over another because they do not stand to gain personally from any specific recommendation. These planners therefore suggest no-load mutual funds or low-load life insurance policies that you probably would never hear about from a commission-oriented planner. Appendix B offers some resources for finding such planners.

Tollbooth Option #3: Fee and Commission. The majority of financial planners charge some sort of fee for providing a financial plan but make most of their income from commissions on the products they sell. In some cases, such planners are actually captives of one company, so they recommend only its product line. Other such planners are independent and therefore recommend the mutual funds or insurance policies of a large number of companies with which they affiliate. However, because your planner earns most of their living by *selling* something to you, consider any advice warily, and try to determine a way to accomplish the same goals with lower-priced products. Always consider total cost.

A variation on this form of compensation is called *fee offset,* meaning that any commission revenue your planner earns from selling you products reduces the fee you pay for planning. If you buy so many products that your entire fee is covered, you deserve a refund or credit of the fee you paid for your basic plan.

Tollbooth Option #4: Salary. Many banks, credit unions, savings and loans, and other organizations that offer financial planning provide the service through a salaried planner. Although these planners do not have as strong an incentive to sell products as do commission-oriented planners, they still

Dear Callie,

I met with a lawyer yesterday to update my will. I still can't believe George is gone, but I knew I had to take care of this in case anything happens to me. I need to feel secure that the kids are provided for.

The lawyer was wonderful: we reviewed everything George and I had decided together, just a few years ago, when we first made our wills. I reiterated our choice of my friend Jennifer to be the legal guardian of the kids (and I checked with her again to make sure she was still willing; she assured me she loves my twins, and since her own kids are older, she said it would be no problem if, God forbid, I die young, too). And I reaffirmed that my brother Andrew would be the executor of my estate. I love both my brothers, but Andrew is better at handling money and details.

It was hard to do all this——especially when I feel sometimes that I can barely get through the day. But I feel so relieved that this is settled. You never know what can happen. Still, I know better days are coming …

—Lisa

steer you toward products offered by their financial institution, on which the institution earns a sales commission. (After all, if most of the salaried planner's clients execute their advice outside the bank or other financial institution, the planner probably will not keep their job for very long.)

Make a Few Pit Stops

Insure Your Assets

Now that you've updated your will and started to do some long-term financial planning, either for your retirement or other major future expenditures (like your children's education, if you have kids), you need to make sure that your insurance is up to date and covers all your needs and potential future situations. Again, you want to be sure that you're taken care of and that your kids or other family members don't need to worry about money if something happens to you.

So take a look at all types of insurance. We think of them as five pit stops on the road to protecting your assets: life insurance, health insurance, disability insurance, homeowners insurance, auto insurance, and long-term care insurance. Let's take the first road: life insurance.

▶ Pit Stop #1: Update Your Life Insurance

The premise behind any kind of life insurance, whether it is a *term* or a *cash-value policy,* is that the surviving spouse and/or family will need the insurance proceeds to replace the insured spouse's income or services (for example, for a stay-at-home mom or dad, how much will it cost to hire someone to care for your children, cook, clean, chauffer, coach, and so on). So before you even do anything with your own life insurance, you need to make certain that you've collected the proceeds on individual and/or group and association policies that covered your spouse, as well as term policies provided by his or her employer. (You must also make sure your own coverage is complete and up to date.)

When you receive the insurance proceeds, invest the money extremely carefully because it must help support you for the rest of your life. You may receive the proceeds in a lump sum, in installments for the remainder of your life, or in payments for a specific number of years. If you take the lump sum, do not rush into any investment even though you may find several financial advisors eager to tell you how to invest the money in return for fees and commissions. Diversify among several investments, some providing high income and others offering more growth potential.

The younger you are when you lost your spouse, the longer you may need to live on the insurance money. If you are in your 60s, and you don't have pension but do have Social Secuirty, invest about half of your portfolio in high-quality stocks or stock mutual funds, which will provide capital growth, as well as current income. Invest the remaining half in fixed-income instruments, such as CDs, bonds, and bond mutual funds, to provide the highest current income with the least risk.

If you have little investment experience, consider buying an *annuity* with the insurance proceeds. This annuity could pay you a fixed monthly amount for the rest of your life so you would not have to worry about investing the money. Compare several insurance companies' payout policies before you settle on an annuity. Appendix B lists resources for finding out more about various insurance companies.

If you are a widow or widower who works and has children, you also should maintain your own life insurance. When you die, the insurance proceeds could go either directly to your children or to a trust on your children's behalf. Your dependent children would need the insurance proceeds to support themselves until they finish their education and become self-supporting. Whether you purchase *term* or *cash-value insurance* depends on how much coverage you need, your age, and how high a premium you can afford.

Stop #1: How Much Should You Buy?

If your family or other people depend on your income, you need life insurance to help replace your income when you pass away. The insurance contract requires that the insurance company pay your beneficiaries a set amount, called the *death benefit,* if you should die for almost any reason. (For example, suicide is usually excluded for the first two years of a policy.) Your beneficiaries can receive the money in one lump sum, free of federal income taxes. The funds should be enough to replace your paycheck for a certain number of years, cover daily living expenses, and pay your final medical bills and burial costs. In addition, the insurance proceeds should provide income for other needs such as estate taxes and college costs.

The key question in buying life insurance is how much coverage your beneficiaries really need. You should determine this before you listen to insurance agents' sometimes confusing pitches or the details of different policies. Unfortunately, assessing how much is enough is not a simple process because each family is different. No general formula exists. You will require more coverage if you have several young children than you will if you have only one child.

The first step in determining your ideal amount of insurance is to examine your current family situation and your potential family situation. If you have minor children, you will need a significant amount of life insurance. Because your children depend on you totally for both short- and long-term expenses, life insurance proceeds should replace your income. Also, if you are the sole owner of a small business or are in partnership with someone else, your life insurance proceeds should replace your income for your family and enable your partner to carry on with the business. A special arrangement called a *buy/sell agreement* can be funded with life insurance proceeds to smooth the transition for both your family and your partner.

In contrast, if you are already retired and/or have no children or have adult, self-supporting children, you probably have a much lower need for life insurance. As you can see, the common thread in determining need in all of these situations is whether survivors will have enough money to maintain their quality of life when you, the insured, die. Calculating how much insurance you need is where this whole process can get very complicated. For an exhaustive analysis, consult an independent insurance agent, or check out one of the resources listed in Appendix B.

Tollbooth 4.1

What Your Estate Will Need to Pay the Bills

Expense	$ Amount
Federal Estate Taxes	$ _____
State Death Taxes	_____
Probate Costs and Attorney Fees	_____
Funeral Expenses	_____
Unreimbursed Medical Costs (for deceased's last illness)	_____
Other (specify) _____	_____
TOTAL IMMEDIATE EXPENSES	$ _____

No matter what route you take, start by using the death expense worksheet in Tollbooth 4.1. Total the immediate expenses your family would incur if you were to die today. We know this is unpleasant to consider, but it's more important than ever, now that you are the sole supporter of your family.

Next, determine your family's ongoing future income and expenses if you were to die. The worksheet in Tollbooth 4.2 provides you with space to record one year's net cash flow, but you must project this amount many years into the future if your family is young. When calculating income, include any benefits your family might be entitled to due to your death, from government programs such as Social Security and veteran's survivor's programs, as well as from life insurance provided by your employer. (Appendix B offers resources to contact to find out how much these programs pay.) Also, you can use the cash flow worksheet you completed in Chapter 2 as a guide in completing the survivor's worksheet in Tollbooth 4.2.

After you complete the worksheet in Tollbooth 4.2, combine your total immediate expenses with your total net cash flow to see how great a gap exists between your expenses and your income. *This gap is what your life insurance should fill.* Depending on your life situation, you will probably discover that this gap is larger than you thought it would be.

Tollbooth 4.2

Survivor's Worksheet

Income	Annual $ Amount
Benefits Income	
Life Insurance	$_____
Pensions	_____
Social Security	_____
Trusts	_____
Veterans	_____
Other	_____
Investment Income	
Annuities	_____
Dividends (from stocks, mutual funds)	_____
Interest (from bank accounts, bonds, mutual funds)	_____
Rent (from owned real estate)	_____
Other	_____
Survivor's Salary	_____
Other Income	_____
TOTAL ANNUAL INCOME	$_____
Expenses	
Child Care	$_____
Children's Education	_____
Clothing	_____
Entertainment and Recreation	_____
Food	
At Home	_____
Outside the Home	_____
Housing	
Mortgage	_____
Rent	_____
Utilities	_____
Other	_____

Insurance Premiums
Auto   _____
Disability   _____
Health   _____
Life   _____
Other   _____

Loan Repayments   _____

Medical and Dental   _____

Taxes
Federal Income   _____
State Income   _____
Local Income   _____
Property   _____
Other   _____

Transportation   _____

Other Expenses   _____

TOTAL ANNUAL EXPENSES $_____

Total Annual Income $_____

Minus Total Annual Expenses $(_____)

Equals

TOTAL NET CASH FLOW $_____

Some simple rules of thumb can give you an idea of how much life insurance you need. At the least, you probably need seven to ten times your annual income; at the most, ten times. Many people require at least $250,000 of coverage, and most need several hundred thousand dollars more if they truly want to cover all of the immediate and future expenses (for the desired number of years) listed above and in the survivor's worksheet shown in Tollbooth 4.2.

Stop #2: Select Which Type of Life Insurance Is Best for You

Now that you have determined how much insurance you need, consider the pros and cons of the four basic types of coverage: *term, whole life, universal life,* and *variable life.* The debates about which type is best will rage forever among financial advisors. You must decide what is best for you based on how much coverage you need, how much premium you can afford, and whether you want insurance only for its death benefit or also for its savings potential. Term insurance merely pays off if you die; whole life, universal life, and variable life insurance are versions of *cash-value insurance,* which combines a death benefit and an investment fund.

Okay, now let's look at the four types of life insurance so you can determine which will be best for your beneficiaries: term insurance and the three types of cash-value insurance (again, whole life, universal life, and variable life insurance).

Term Insurance. Term insurance offers financial protection on your life for a specified and finite period of time, usually one, five, 10, or 20 years. The only way your term policy will pay out is if you die during this period. In this case, your beneficiaries will probably be offered a lump-sum payout or a series of annuity payments.

When the period expires, you can usually renew the policy, though at a higher premium because you are older and statistically more likely to die. If your policy offers a *guaranteed renewability feature,* you do not have to take a medical test or otherwise prove insurability to continue coverage for another term. You can also buy term insurance that provides a *convertibility feature,* which allows you to convert some or all of the coverage into whole life insurance without a medical exam. If you stop paying premiums on a term policy, your coverage ceases.

You can purchase far more protection for your dollar with term insurance than you can with a cash-value policy. Term insurance is therefore ideal if you have a large insurance need for a specific period of time. For example, you might need coverage for the years before your children become self-supporting, which should be in their mid-20s.

The chief advantage of term insurance is that it is very inexpensive. Hundreds of companies offer term; therefore, the market is extremely competitive. Appendix B offers suggestions for where you can obtain price quotes on term coverage.

Make sure the policy you buy is not only low priced but also backed by a financially strong insurance company. Preferably, the carrier should have at least an A rating from two or three of the major ratings agencies.

You may be able to get a good deal by buying more group term through your employer's plan, though you should compare those premium prices carefully with premiums on policies that you can obtain on your own. You may also be able to obtain a good group term policy through a trade association, an alumni group, or another organization to which you belong. However, if you change jobs or drop your membership in the trade association or alumni group, you may lose your coverage. Strongly consider purchasing a policy of your own instead.

The disadvantage of term insurance is that the premium rises over time. As mentioned earlier, your premium stays the same during the term of a policy but increases each time you renew. This is because your chance of dying becomes greater as you age, and the insurance company needs to collect a higher premium to offset the greater risk of having to pay a claim. Term premiums rise slowly while you are in your 20s and 40s but start to get much more expensive as you progress through your 50s and 60s. By the time you reach your 70s, term insurance is astronomically expensive and probably could be dropped.

Cash-Value Insurance. Instead of buying term insurance, which offers pure protection, you can choose to purchase one of several varieties of cash-value insurance. All of these policies (again, whole life, universal life, or variable life) add a tax-deferred savings feature to the insurance protection component of the policy. Let's look at each.

Whole life insurance. Whole life insurance, often called *straight life* or *permanent insurance* by agents, is the opposite of term. Whereas term insurance starts with low premiums that rise over time upon renewal and provides you with no investment reserves, whole life locks in for life one premium rate, part of which is invested for your benefit. However, whole life premiums are much more expensive than term premiums.

Whole life remains in force as long as you live and pay your premiums. You need not renew it, as you do term life insurance. The younger you are when you buy a whole life policy, the lower your lifelong premiums. The insurance company uses your premium dollars to cover three expenses: death claims, administrative costs, and investments. Most of your money ends up invested in stocks, bonds, real estate, and other capital assets that can appreciate and produce income over time. The cash value that your whole life policy accumulates results from those investments that are paid in the form of policy dividends, minus death claims and administrative expenses.

As bond rates fell in the 1990s, yields on insurance portfolios also started to recede from their high of 8–12 percent in the 1980s, but at a much slower pace than returns on portfolios holding shorter term money-market instruments. All whole life policies, however, make a minimum earnings guarantee, usually of about 3 to 4 percent.

Universal life insurance. This form of cash-value insurance offers much more flexibility than traditional whole life policies. If you choose this type of life insurance, you can pay premiums at any time and in any amount, as long as you meet certain minimum levels. Also, you can easily increase or decrease the amount of your insurance protection to meet your current needs. In addition, you can always tell exactly how much of your premium dollar is allocated to insurance protection, administrative expenses, and savings. These figures are never clearly disclosed when you own a whole life policy.

Unlike whole life premiums (which are invested in long-term bonds and mortgages), universal life premiums reflect the current short-term rates available in the money markets. (This type of insurance was created in the high-interest-rate years of the early 1980s, and it offered policyholders very high rates of return from investments in money-market instruments. When rates dropped by the 1990s, universal life became much less popular.) Insurance companies set a rate of return for one year, then readjust the yield up or down, depending on the level of interest rates. However, universal life policies guarantee a minimum yield of about 3 percent or 4 percent.

A final advantage of universal life therefore is that the returns you earn on your cash value will reflect a sharp upturn in interest rates far more quickly than the returns on a traditional whole life policy. However, if rates fall or remain depressed, you may have to settle for lower returns for many years.

Variable life insurance. If you are willing to take higher risks in search of better returns, variable life insurance offers the option of investing your cash value in stock, bond, or money-market funds managed by the insurance company. As with other cash-value policies, these returns compound tax deferred until you withdraw your principal. A good fund manager operating in a bull market can easily provide double-digit gains and outperform a traditional whole-life portfolio. But markets do not always rise, and this year's hero can become next year's goat. You have the option of shifting your money among stocks, bonds, and cash vehicles, but the chances of selling at just the right moment are remote.

Your investment timing affects not only the appreciation or depreciation of your cash value in a variable life policy. The death benefit also rises and falls based on investment performance. However, the death benefit will never drop below the original amount of insurance coverage for which you contracted.

Because the stock, bond, and money-market funds within variable insurance policies are legally considered securities, the life insurance agent who sells you a policy must be a licensed registered representative of a broker-dealer. The agent must give you a prospectus, as with any investment, and explain the risks as well as the potential rewards of the plan, in addition to the costs.

When choosing a variable life policy, study the long-term track record of the funds offered. It is very difficult and expensive to switch out of one variable contract and into another under the management of a new insurance company if performance starts to lag.

Accelerated Death Benefit Insurance. This is a newer type of life insurance policy, also called *living benefits policies.* These policies allow you, in particular cases, to access your death benefit while you are still living. These policies usually will make payments while you are alive under these three circumstances:

1. If you need long-term care, either in a nursing home or at home;
2. If you are struck by a catastrophic illness or disease that runs up enormous medical bills. The policy lists specific diseases and surgeries covered, most commonly heart attacks, strokes, life-threatening cancers, coronary-artery bypass surgeries, renal failures, paralyses, and major organ transplants; or
3. If you are diagnosed as terminally ill. If your doctor confirms in writing that you have only weeks or months to live, you can tap your death benefit. Remember, however, that if you withdraw part or all of your death benefit while you are still living, your beneficiaries receive less when you die.

Comparing Term and Cash-Value Life Insurance. When you understand the differences between term and the myriad forms of cash-value life insurance, you must decide which is best for you. Some people believe that you come out ahead if you buy the cheapest, highest quality term policy you can find and invest the difference between the term premium and the premium that you would pay on cash-value insurance in stocks, bonds, and mutual funds of your choice. Indeed, if you actually follow through on this strategy and build a sizable portfolio on your own through a disciplined savings regimen, you probably would come out ahead. By the time you retire, you not only would have had the insurance coverage you needed at a low price, but you also would have avoided paying the high commission charges wrapped into a cash-value policy.

On the other hand, proponents of cash-value insurance say that, as well intentioned as most people might be, they do not, in fact, exercise the discipline to invest the difference between premiums every year for the long term. The higher premiums you would pay into a cash-value policy are therefore a form of forced savings. In addition, the cash value accumulates tax deferred, whereas your personal investments are subject to yearly taxation unless they occur within an individual retirement account (IRA), a Keogh account, a salary reduction plan, or another tax-deferred plan. You do not have to opt for only term or only cash-value life insurance. Your best choice might be to put together a combined policy that gives you adequate protection from term but also builds investment reserves from cash-value insurance. If your salary rises over time and you feel you can afford it, convert some of the term into cash-value insurance.

Annuities. In addition to term and cash-value life insurance, insurance companies sell annuities. Although annuities are issued by life insurance companies, they work quite differently than cash-value or term insurance policies. Annuities pay a regular stream of income while you live, usually after you retire, and are more like investments than life insurance, which pays your beneficiaries a lump sum or an annual or monthly income when you die. Annuities also provide the advantage of tax-deferred compounding on the investment portion of the account.

The two basic kinds of annuities are:

1. *Immediate annuities* are purchased with a lump sum (and begin to generate an income stream immediately). Typically, they are purchased by people in retirement to provide a guaranteed stream of income. The

lump sum might come from a distribution by a salary reduction plan, an IRA, a Keogh plan, or investments that you have built up over the years. Different insurance companies offer varying levels of monthly income, depending on how long you will receive payments.

2. *Deferred annuities* are typically bought by younger people who want to defer taxes for many years, then convert to a payout schedule once they retire. You can purchase a flexible premium retirement annuity through regular monthly or annual deposits of as little as $25. You are not required to pay a premium every year, but the more you invest, the greater your annuity's value grows. You can also buy an annuity with one lump sum. This is called a *single-premium deferred annuity* (SPDA). Most companies require at least $2,500, though they prefer $10,000 or more. Annuities also have a life insurance component because your beneficiaries receive the entire accumulated value of your annuity (what you paid in plus the interest earned) if you die before receiving annuity payments.

If your life insurance policy accumulates enough cash value, you can convert that value into an annuity to boost your income stream in retirement. Take this step, however, only if your children are self-supporting and you no longer need as much life insurance.

Fixed Versus Variable Annuities. You have two annuity options:

1. *Fixed-dollar Annuity:* This is the more conservative route, because the insurance company invests in bonds or mortgages. Each year, the company announces the *fixed return* for the next year, depending on the current investment portfolio. The fixed return is the rate the company will credit to your annuity. During the early 2000s, rates dropped to the 5 to 6 percent range. The insurance company provides some level of guaranteed minimum return, usually about 3 to 4 percent.

Do not be lured by a high first-year rate, which often drops dramatically in subsequent years. To protect yourself, make sure that your policy offers a *bail-out provision*. This gives you the right to liquidate all or part of your annuity without cost if your renewal rate is ever less than 1 percent of the previously offered rate. Usually, you must notify the insurance company within 30 days of receiving notice of the renewal rate that you plan to bail out. Nevertheless, do not rely on the bail-out clause if you opt for a fixed annuity. Choose a company that has paid a consistently competitive return; chances are that its record will continue.

2. *A variable annuity*: This option offers the potential for higher returns, though at greater risk, because it gives you a choice among several stock, bond, and money-market portfolios. Within the stock category, you will normally be offered a selection of sector, aggressive growth, growth, growth and income, international, and balanced funds. With bonds, you may shift among corporate, government, high-yield, and international fixed-income portfolios. You can allocate your money among stock and bond options any way you like and transfer the funds as market conditions change. As the stock and bond markets swing in value over the years, your annuity's value also rises and falls.

If you select a company with a proven investment performance, you can probably do far better in the long term with a variable annuity than with a fixed-dollar annuity. The key is to purchase a contract with top-notch investment managers. Appendix B lists various publications that can help you find such annuities. Because it is difficult and expensive to switch from one company's variable annuity to another's, you should research your decision carefully.

Payout options. Once you reach retirement age, annuities offer many different payout options. In general, the longer you obligate the company to pay benefits, the lower your monthly check. Whether you think that you will live a short or a long time determines your regular stipend. Each company determines its payout scale by estimating survival rates and the company's expected earnings on investments. The duration of annuity payments can be based on a life contingency, a certain period of time, or on a combination of the two. The usual choices you will be offered include a 10-year term certain annuity, a life annuity with 10-year term certain, a life annuity, or a joint and survivor annuity, so ask about all of these when you do the research.

Once you start receiving payouts from annuities, you must pay income tax on a portion of those payouts. Each payment is considered part investment earnings and part return of your original principal. You must pay tax on the investment earnings but not on the return of capital. The insurance company informs you how much of each payment constitutes earnings and principal.

Unless you absolutely need access to your annuity money before retirement, don't touch it. If you take distributions from your annuity before age

59½, you not only must pay income tax on the earnings but you also owe the IRS a stiff 10 percent early withdrawal penalty. The only ways around this penalty before age 59½ are if you suffer a long-term disability or if you die and the annuity proceeds are distributed to your beneficiaries.

Fees and Expenses. Finally, pay careful attention to the several fees attached to every annuity contract. Most companies do not explicitly charge an up-front commission, or load. Instead, they levy a hefty *surrender charge* of as much as 10 percent of your principal if you want to transfer your annuity to another company within the first five or 10 years of the contract. On the other hand, many annuities offer a free withdrawal provision after the first year and for every year thereafter that surrender charges apply. This allows you to withdraw a certain percent (usually up to 10 percent) of the accumulated account value. (Prior to age 59½, these partial withdrawals would be subject to penalty tax.) In addition, most annuity marketers charge annual maintenance fees of $25 to $50 to cover the administrative costs of maintaining an account.

Stop #3: Reduce Your Life Insurance Tolls—How to Minimize Sales Charges and Other Expenses

Whichever type of life insurance policy or annuity contract you choose be particularly wary of high fees and expenses. Some insurers pay their salespeople much higher commissions than others, and you can be sure that those sales charges will come out of your pocket one way or another. Sales commissions usually are not stated explicitly in an insurance contract, but they are most often paid out of your first few years of premiums. High commissions might hit you in the form of slower cash value buildup, reduced dividends, and/or greater expenses.

One way to get around such high fees is to buy from one of the growing number of *low-load or no-load insurance carriers* that sell mostly over the phone and through the mail. A list of some of the larger low-load or no-load companies is provided in Appendix B.

Whenever you purchase a policy, determine the cancellation fees or surrender charges for pulling out of the contract. These fees can be quite high, such as 7 percent of your accumulated cash value, particularly if you want to withdraw in the first few years of your policy. Think long and hard about switching from your current policy to a new one, despite any strong encouragement you receive from an agent. It takes years for your cash value to accumulate significantly, and you can lose a good deal of your investment reserves to fees if you transfer to another policy.

Stop #4: Comparing Costs of Various Life Insurance Policies

When you have narrowed your search for the best policy to a few companies, you can use the *interest-adjusted net cost index* to help you make your final decision. This index, available for both term and cash value policies, factors in all financial elements of an insurance policy, such as the company's dividend record, expenses, premium costs, and timing of payments. The result allows you to compare the price of policies, all things being equal.

The index is expressed as a cost per $1,000 of insurance. For example, a policy with a $5 cost index costs $5 per $1,000 of coverage per year, or $500 for a $100,000 policy. These index costs range from a low of about $1 to as much as $10. Ask your agent for this cost index on two or more comparable policies, though that data may not be volunteered eagerly. The lower the cost index, the more insurance your money buys. (See Appendix B for where to obtain this data.)

While you size up the insurer, the insurer also evaluates you as a potential risk. On the insurance application form, it asks your family medical history, occupation, age, sex, and health habits (such as smoking or drinking), as well as other factors that affect your chances of living a long time. The insurer may even ask you to undergo a medical exam from a doctor of the company's choosing. Once it compiles your profile, the insurance company rates you according to the following risk levels:

▶ *Preferred risks* have the least likelihood of dying prematurely and therefore pay the lowest rates.

▶ *Standard risks* are a bit more likely to die early because of health problems and therefore pay higher rates than preferred risks.

▶ *Substandard risks* are those who smoke, drink, are overweight, and have a history of medical problems in their families. As a result, they pay high rates for coverage.

Last Stop, so Pull Over: Choosing a Life Insurance Company

Because life insurance is a long-term commitment, you want to make sure that the company you choose will be around years from now to fulfill its part of the bargain. Therefore, examine a company's financial strength ratings as published by A.M. Best, Standard & Poor's, Moody's, Duff & Phelps, and Weiss Research. Also, evaluate the service you receive from the company's representatives. After you buy your policy, you probably will not have much contact with your agent, but they should be able to answer questions knowledgeably and readily. For example, if your family situation changes, you might wonder how your need for insurance changes. The agent should go over the insurance contract with you carefully so you understand its key clauses and your options.

▶ Pit Stop #2: Update Your Health Insurance

Having access to good health insurance is crucial. Depending on your spouse's employer's policy, your health insurance premiums may or may not be paid by your spouse's employer after your spouse dies.

Under COBRA (the Congressional Omnibus Budget Reconciliation Act), you and your dependent children must be permitted to continue group coverage for three years after your spouse dies at the same price your spouse's employer would have paid for coverage, plus a small fee for administration. Although you gain the advantage of group rates, you still have to pay the health insurance premium, which you might not have had to do when your spouse was alive. If you haven't done so already, be sure to contact your spouse's employer to find out more about the COBRA benefits to which you are entitled.

If you cannot obtain coverage through your spouse's employer, try to sign on with a managed care program, an HMO (health maintenance organization), or a PPO (preferred provider organization) during one of their open enrollment periods. If you can't secure coverage with such an organization, you might have to buy an individual policy through a company like Blue Cross/Blue Shield during one of its open enrollment periods.

Five Routes to Health Insurance

Although the common types of insurance programs have been around for years, if you're unfamiliar with them or unclear on the differences between then, the following sections offer a quick refresher course. For more information, talk to your employer's human resources department or your financial advisor.

Route #1: Traditional Health Insurance Programs. The optimal traditional fee-for-service indemnity policy is divided into two plans:

1. The *basic plan* reimburses you for doctors' bills, drugs, outpatient surgical procedures, and other medical expenses up to a certain annual dollar limit.
2. The second plan, called *major medical,* covers extended hospital visits and other major medical procedures.

If these plans are offered by your employer, both types will usually cover you (the employee), your spouse (should you decide to remarry), and any children age 23 or younger if they attend school.

The basic plan, which may be offered directly by your employer (if you're currently working) or by an outside insurance company, usually applies deductibles of $100 to $1,000 or more before your bills are reimbursed. Some companies impose a fixed annual deductible of $100 or $200 for all employees; others tie the deductible to your salary level. After you pay the deductible out of your pocket, all further bills are usually reimbursed for 80 percent of your cost, up to a specified annual limit. Once you have spent more than that limit, you are reimbursed 100 percent.

Some basic plans are far less generous than others. Depending on the company you work for and the insurance carrier, reimbursement for some procedures might be limited or omitted altogether. This includes such expenses as home health care, dentist bills, psychiatric care, and drug or alcohol abuse treatment.

Your major medical plan normally pays 100 percent of the cost of a semi-private hospital room up to a certain length of time, such as 120 days. After that time limit, the plan typically covers 80 percent of your bills. Hospitalization charges usually include room and board, nursing care, drugs, medical devices, food, and fees for specialists, such as surgeons, who work in the hospital. If your surgery can be performed on an outpatient basis, these expenses are also usually covered. Most major medical policies have a lifetime cap, typically $1 million. Some major medical plans, such as those offered by Blue Cross and Blue Shield, require you to cover the first $2,000 to $5,000 worth of hospital costs as a deductible before they pay hospital bills directly. This stipulation is often called the *stop-loss clause* because it limits your loss to the deductible. You are responsible for the initial deductible (say $250) after which the insurer will pay 80 percent of the covered medical costs, and you will pay 20 percent. When your total out-of-pocket expenditures reach a certain amount, such as $2,000, the insurer pays 100 percent.

If you want or feel you need even more insurance protection, you can buy additional major medical coverage to supplement a regular major medical policy with a low lifetime limit. *Excess major medical policies,* often called *catastrophic policies,* usually have a very high deductible of about $15,000, but they can be vital if you need an expensive medical procedure.

Route #2: HMOs. Instead of choosing your own doctors and getting reimbursed for expenses under the traditional fee-for-service health insurance plan, you might consider an HMO. There are hundreds of HMOs across the country that offer full medical services for a flat annual fee, which you pay on monthly installments. That fee might be several hundred or several thousand dollars, depending on the HMO, your employer, and the plan coverage.

When you become an HMO member, you have unlimited access to the organization's medical services. You can visit a doctor for preventive check-ups, minor problems, or emergencies, sometimes for a small fee of $5 or $10 per visit. If the HMO runs a central medical facility, you must go there for all procedures. However, if you are out of town, the HMO will reimburse you for visits to approved doctors or hospitals. In a true life-or-death emergency, you can go to any hospital and still get reimbursed.

An HMO offers several advantages, the most important being your total out-of-pocket costs are limited to the annual HMO fee, plus small charges for special services. Because the HMO charges group rates, the premium will be less than the fee you normally would pay for traditional insurance coverage. In addition, you no longer must deal with deductibles, co-payments, or coverage limits. And neither must you search for a generalist or specialist practitioner because the HMO employs every type of physician you probably will ever need. If you have an extremely rare condition that no one on the HMO's staff can handle, the HMO will locate a specialist for you. You will also receive prescription drugs either free of charge or at very low cost because the HMO buys them at bulk prices directly from manufacturers. Finally, all of your medical records are kept in one place, so your medical history is immediately available to whatever doctor treats you.

If HMOs offer so many advantages, why doesn't everyone join one? What you gain in financial control, you lose in medical choice, in the following ways:

► You cannot bring your existing doctor to the HMO, so you must choose a new primary care physician from a list provided by the HMO.

► If your chosen doctor is not available on the day you visit the clinic, you must see whoever is working.

► If you need a specialist, you must select one from the HMO's approved list, regardless of whether that's the best person in town.

► In addition, many HMO generalists hate to refer patients to specialists because it costs the HMO more, and one of the main goals of HMOs is to control costs.

► Some HMOs also have a reputation for discouraging medical tests.

► Also, services such as vision, hearing, and dental care and psychiatric treatment are considered basic in some HMO plans but not all.

► The same lack of choice applies to hospitals: You go where the HMO sends you, not where you might prefer. If you seek help at a hospital not specifically authorized by your HMO, you will probably have to pay the entire bill on your own.

Therefore, before you join an HMO, ask plenty of questions. Following are a few areas to explore:

► What kinds of experiences have other insured patients had with the plan?

► How competent are the doctors? What percentage of doctors are board-certified? (The more doctors who are *board-certified,* meaning that they successfully passed a specialty test, the better. The average certification rate is about 70 percent.)

► How long do patients wait for an appointment to see a specialist?

► Is preventive medicine encouraged or discouraged? If encouraged, specifically what does the HMO do to minimize medical problems?

► How are HMO members treated at HMO-affiliated hospitals?

► Is the HMO accredited? (This is not required, but it is certainly better to join an accredited HMO than an unaccredited one. Agencies such as the National Committee for Quality Assurance set the most stringent standards.)

► Is there a high staff turnover rate at the HMO you are interested in? (A high rate can mean that the patient load is too large and that doctors are unhappy.)

▶ What is the member retention rate? (A higher rate indicates a better level of member satisfaction. Good HMOs conduct annual patient surveys. Review them to gain insight into member satisfaction.)

Appendix B lists resources to help you evaluate managed care plans.

Route #3: PPOs. Somewhere between the traditional fee-for-service plan and the HMO is the PPO (preferred provider organization). Under this type of insurance, your employer, union or health insurance company enlists the services of generalist and specialist doctors, hospitals, and many other health care providers. These caregivers receive a set monthly fee to provide a set level of services. If they give more care than was agreed on, they earn more money.

Route #4. Medicare/Medigap Insurance. If you're age 65 or older, Medicare provides substantial health insurance benefits—whether you are retired or still working.

Medicare is designed to cover part of your expenses for short-term acute medical problems rather than long-term conditions requiring custodial care. It pays for hospitalization, surgery, doctor bills, home health care, and skilled nursing care considered to be medically necessary and within reasonable cost limits.

Medicare coverage is divided into two parts:

1. *Medicare Part A* is primarily hospital insurance. If you are eligible, you can enroll without charge; however, if you are not covered by Social Security, you must pay part of the premium. When you apply for Social Security benefits, you automatically apply for Medicare. If you plan to work past age 65, you should still apply for Medicare at age 65. Medicare Part A covers expenses for hospitalization, nursing-home care, home health care, hospice care, and blood transfusions.

2. *Medicare Part B* is a medical insurance program covering charges from doctors, surgeons, and other outpatient providers, as well as fees for medical supplies. Part B is optional if you are eligible for Part A. To take advantage of Part B, you must enroll and pay a monthly premium. Medicare Part B covers expenses for medical services, tests (e.g., lab work), home health care services, outpatient hospital care, and blood transfusions.

For more details on the expenses Medicare covers, as well as the cost of deductibles, co-payments, and premiums, see Appendix B.

You should also keep in mind that Medicare excludes many medical expenses, for example, you will not be reimbursed for the following:

► Nursing care beyond 100 days in a skilled-nursing facility; private nursing care; and any care in a center not approved by Medicare
► Custodial and intermediate nursing care
► Routine physicals, dentistry, acupuncture, immunizations, cosmetic surgery, and foot, eye, and hearing care
► Doctor charges that exceed approved Medicare levels or that Medicare does not consider medically necessary. Each year, the government publishes a fee schedule listing maximum Medicare payments, which are usually far less than doctors charge regular commercial patients.
► Care in foreign countries, except in certain limited circumstances in Canada and Mexico.

Because Medicare coverage is limited in so many ways, several plans have been designed to fill in the gaps. These plans are called *Medigap* policies and are discussed in more detail in the next section.

Route #5: Specialized Health Insurance Policies. In addition to the usual health insurance plans, several more specialized policies are marketed aggressively; you should know something about these so that you don't invest in unnecessary or inappropriate health insurance. Make sure you know what you're getting, and don't make any hasty decisions at this vulnerable time of your life.

Hospital indemnity plans. The most widely advertised policies are hospital indemnity plans, which pay a specified amount of cash each day that you are hospitalized. The plans are usually advertised on television or through the mail. Such pitches announce that you can get $75 a day, for example, while paying only pennies in premiums.

The problem with these plans is that hospitals charge an average of $750 a day (in other words, *10 times* what the plan covers), and most of the hospital's services are *already covered* by your comprehensive health insurance plan. In addition, hospital indemnity plans often limit pre-existing conditions, which may prevent you from receiving any benefits at all. Also, most plans also have elimination periods, meaning that you must be hospitalized for a certain number of days before you can even collect benefits. Nowadays, most hospitals try to shorten patients' stays, so it can be very difficult to collect on these policies.

Long-term care policies. Such policies cover the health costs of long-term custodial care either in a nursing home or at home. Although the coverage from long-term care policies can offset some of the costs of such care, they rarely pay all the bills. For example, nursing homes charge between $60,000 and $150,000 a year, and home health aides can cost between $10,000 and $20,000 a year for three visits a week. Weigh this against what long-term care policies pay, which is between $75 and $150 a day for nursing homes and 50 to 100 percent of that amount for at-home care. Therefore, even though some policies offer inflation-adjustment clauses, you should consider these policies as a *supplement* to, not a *replacement* for, more comprehensive policies. (And for a more detailed look at the best long-term health care solutions, see Appendix B.)

Medicare supplement policies. Known as *Medigap plans,* these policies are designed to pick up where Medicare leaves off (as mentioned above), covering Medicare co-payments and deductibles. Some supplemental policies also pay for products and services not covered by Medicare. As long as you enroll in Medicare Part B within six months after enrolling in Medicare Part A, you cannot be rejected when you apply for a Medicare supplement policy if you are at least 65 years old. Currently, 10 standard Medicare supplement policies exist, labeled *A* through *J* for easier comparison. Policy A is the most basic and is available to all Medicare recipients. Policies B through J offer more and more benefits, and more and more people are excluded from qualification.

All 10 Medigap policies cover at least the daily coinsurance amount for hospitalization under Medicare Part A. The more inclusive policies pay additional benefits for such services as preventive medical care, coverage in a foreign country, hospice care, prescription drugs, or home visits—all of which Medicare does not cover.

A newer form of Medicare supplement insurance is called *Medicare Select.* It is a form of private Medigap insurance designed to be less costly to policyholders because policyholders must use a designated group of health care professionals and facilities. The insurance company selects the providers, which may include HMOs and PPOs. The medical service providers offer discount prices because they are assured a steady flow of patients.

When shopping for a Medigap policy, watch for pre-existing conditions clauses that preclude you from receiving benefits if you already have developed an ailment. Also, make sure that your policy is guaranteed renewable. Finally, you should examine the elimination periods imposed for hospital stays. You may have to be hospitalized several days before benefits kick in, which may mean that you may never collect a dime.

The process of choosing a Medigap policy can be quite complex and confusing.

Many people are pressured into making quick decisions by commission-hungry salespeople. Instead, take your time, and make sure that you understand exactly what you are buying. Don't make a common mistake and purchase too much insurance; one comprehensive Medigap plan should be all you need. According to federal law, even after you buy a policy, you have 30 days to review it and obtain a full refund of all premiums paid.

Specific disease policies. Also known as *dread disease policies,* these policies play on people's fears by covering a specific disease, most commonly cancer. These pay limited benefits if you contract the illness named in the policy, and each policy established establishes a strict definition of a specific disease, which limits your ability to collect. For example, health problems caused by cancer usually don't entitle you to benefits.

As with hospital indemnity coverage, a good comprehensive policy costs far less money for the benefits they provide than a disease-specific plan. In some states, insurance regulators have prohibited the sale of cancer insurance, because the questionable sales practices they could invite that take advantage of people's fears of this disease.

▶ Pit Stop #3: Update Your Disability and Long-Term Care Insurance

In addition to your overall health insurance, disability insurance may be even more important to you when you lose your spouse or are on your own and still need to earn a paycheck.

Do Not Pass "Go" Without Collecting $200: Your Spouse's Disability Insurance

If your spouse was disabled and received disability payments, those payments stopped at death, thus depriving you of that regular source of income. Your spouse might also have received Social Security disability payments. After your spouse's death, these benefits will be changed to survivor's benefits once you provide the Social Security Administration with a valid death certificate. Once you turn 65, the disability payments will be converted into Social Security retirement benefits. The Social Security Administration has established many complex rules regarding the amount of disability benefits that widows and widowers receive, depending on their situation and age. See Appendix B for where to call for more details on disability insurance.

Check Your Air Bag: Get Your Own Disability Insurance

Your own disability insurance is vital for widows and widowers who still work. Because you are the only person supporting yourself and any dependent children, you need to be protected in case you become seriously injured or ill. The best way to purchase disability insurance is through your employer, though you can also buy it from most major insurance companies.

Although you might think it highly unlikely that you will ever become disabled, either on the job or outside of work, you should know that, according to the Health Insurance Association of America, at age 40, for example, you have a 19 percent probability of suffering at least one disability lasting more than 90 days. But take heart: the following information describes what type of financial assistance may be available to you if you do become disabled.

If you miss work for a short time, your employer will probably provide short-term sick leave. You might also collect benefits from workers' compensation if you were injured on the job. Other government programs, such as veterans benefits, civil service disability, black lung insurance for miners, and Medicaid for low-income people might also kick in. If you were injured in a car accident, your auto insurance will pay you a certain amount of cash for a limited period of time. And if you are a union member, you might be eligible for group union disability coverage.

You will qualify for Social Security disability benefits if you become severely disabled. How much you receive depends on your salary and the number of years you have been covered by Social Security. Following are the ground rules for receiving Social Security disability payments:

▶ *You must be disabled for at least five months and expect to be out of commission for at least a year, total.* Expect the Social Security Administration to take at least three months to process your claim, so keep in mind that you should file as soon as you think you will be eligible.

▶ The amount you receive from Social Security will be reduced by other payments you get from other government disability programs. For example, any money you receive from military, civil service, or government pensions or from workers' compensation is subtracted from your Social Security benefit. All of these income sources combined cannot exceed 80 percent of your average earnings before you became disabled.

▶ You must not be able to perform any job whatsoever, not just the work you did before you were injured or became ill.

▶ You will qualify for Medicare after receiving Social Security payments for two years. You must enroll and pay the monthly premium to receive both medical and hospital coverage under Medicare.

▶ You must pay federal income tax on your disability benefits if your income exceeds a certain limit. You must pay tax on as much as 85 percent of your benefits if your provisional income, which includes tax-exempt municipal bond interest plus one half of your Social Security benefit, exceeds $34,000.

However, even if you collect from several government programs, you probably will not receive enough money to live comfortably. This is where individual long-term disability insurance becomes crucial. If you qualify, you can receive between 50 and 80 percent of your regular salary, depending on the policy, plus cost-of-living adjustments in some policies. (Companies do not pay 100 percent of your salary because they want you to have an incentive to go back to work.)

▶ Insurance for the Long Haul: Long-Term Care Insurance

You work diligently to accumulate assets that will, you hope, provide a lifetime income and perhaps a legacy for your heirs. An extended stay in a nursing home could destroy that plan. You can transfer all or most of that risk to an insurance company by purchasing long-term care insurance.

Understanding long-term care insurance can be a challenge because each company and policy has its own features and benefits. Long-term care insurance is designed to cover the costs of caring for individuals with one or more chronic health conditions from which they are generally not expected to recover. It is not traditional medical insurance; rather, it covers skilled, intermediate, and custodial types of care, which focus primarily on assistance with activities of daily living or supervision related to cognitive impairment.

To qualify for benefits in most states, you must require substantial assistance with two of six activities of daily living or need substantial supervision due to cognitive impairment. As we mentioned earlier, depending on what state you live in, current care costs can range from $60,000 to $150,000 a year and up. If you're 60 years old today, by the time you're 85, the costs will be closer to $100,000 to $550,000, due to inflation.

People who save to pay for this care will pay for it with after-tax dollars. Medicaid may be an option, but it's only available if you meet very strict requirements.

Long-term care insurance benefits paid by tax-qualified policies that meet government specifications are free from income tax. Also, premiums paid on a tax-qualified policy may be partially deductible as a medical expense under itemized deductions on your income tax return.

You shouldn't purchase long-term care insurance if any of the following conditions apply to your financial situation:

► You truly cannot afford the premium.
► You could not afford a premium increase of 10 to 20 percent.
► You have limited assets.
► You have only Social Security or Supplemental Security Income as an income source.
► You have trouble paying for utilities, rent, food, medicine, or other important needs.
► You can afford and prefer to pay care costs on your own.

On the other hand, you *should* buy long-term care insurance if you want to maintain your independence, retain more control over your care choices and the quality of care, or preserve your income and assets as much as possible. Roadmap 4.1 covers some of the issues you should consider when deciding to buy long-term care insurance.

Learn the Language

Some words to watch for include *substantial assistance* and *substantial supervision*. The more lenient definitions are *standby assistance* for daily living activities and *presence of another individual* for cognitive impairment. More restrictive definitions are *hands-on assistance* for a majority of the time and *verbal supervision and cuing* for a majority of the time, or *continual supervision*. The more restrictive the definition, the harder qualifying for benefits will be.

Finally, look at who determines if you qualify for benefits and develops your plan of care. Many policies require only that a licensed health care practitioner of your choosing certify that you need assistance and will need it for longer than 90 days. A few policies require that a care advisor, employed by the insurance company or by an agency with which the insurance company has a contract, be used. Finally, as with other types of insurance, the company you select should have a top financial rating. It also should have been in the long-term care insurance business for at least 10 years with a good history of paying claims. For more information on buying long-term care insurance, see Appendix B.

▶ Roadside Assistance: Medicaid Decisions for Long-Term Care

Medicaid is a partnership (begun in 1965) between each state and the federal government to provide medical care to the elderly, blind, and disabled poor. Unlike Medicare, eligibility for Medicaid is based on financial need. Medicaid's primary benefit is the safety net it provides for long-term nursing care for those who cannot afford it. Currently, Medicaid covers more than half of the long-term care costs in the United States.

It's an extremely complex system that's handled differently in each state. We can only address the general basics, so check with your state for its unique guidelines. Applications for Medicaid coverage are made with the appropriate state agency. Substantial documentation and paperwork are required.

Following are the basic requirements for Medicaid eligibility:

▶ *U.S. citizenship or qualified alien status.*

▶ *Residency in the state where application is made.*

▶ *Medical need.* You must need long-term care, usually determined by the inability to perform at least two of the six following activities of daily living without assistance:

1. dressing;
2. transferring, such as getting from a bed to a chair;
3. using the bathroom;
4. eating;
5. bathing; and
6. maintaining continence.

▶ *Limited financial resources.* The first of two financial requirements, generally this means that the individual applying for Medicaid cannot have available resources or assets exceeding $2,000. Generally, the following count as exceptions to "available resources":

1. *Home.* It's excluded as long as you intend to return there.
2. *Vehicle.* The maximum exempt value for an automobile is generally $4,500.
3. *Household goods.* These generally are exempt unless they are of unusual value.
4. *Property or tools.* Those used in your trade or business and necessary for support.
5. *Life insurance.* Only policies up to $1,500 are not included. If the total face value is higher, the cash surrender value counts.
6. *Burial plot.* Prepaid burial expenses and an account designated for funeral arrangements are generally allowed up to $1,500.

▶ *Income cap.* Almost half the states have an income cap. It varies, but most states fix it at 300 percent of the current monthly maximum Supplemental Social Security benefit. Other states are "medically needy states," where income eligibility for Medicaid is the inability to pay the actual cost of private care from the income available.

Essentially, to qualify for Medicaid, an individual must exhaust all other assets except for your house, car, and household belongings.

Watch Out for Hazards: What to Look Out for in Disability Insurance Policies

Many clauses in disability contracts can be crucial in determining the benefits you will receive if you are injured. The following paragraphs describe the basics that you should be aware of.

Definition of disability. Some policies pay if you are unable to perform your customary job. Others stipulate that you must be unable to do *any* job before they consider you disabled. Many use a combination of the inability to perform your own job for an initial period (usually the first year of your disability) and then the inability to perform at any job for which you are suited based on your education and experience. Some policies require that you be totally disabled; others pay if you are only partly disabled. So make sure you understand how the policy is really covering you.

Cause of disability. Some policies provide benefits only if you are injured in an accident. Others pay if you become injured or ill. The best policies cover both accidents and illness, and they pay no matter how you become disabled, so look for these.

Exclusions. Insurers usually will not pay disability benefits if an injury is caused by a suicide attempt, drug abuse, a crash of a noncommercial aircraft, military service, or a normal pregnancy.

Residual benefits. Residual benefits are partial benefits. For example, if you are healthy enough to work one day a week or earn 20 percent of your former income by performing less demanding tasks, a policy offering residual benefits will pay you 80 percent of the full benefit. So the more you work, the less residual funds you will receive.

Payment amount. Your monthly benefit is based on your level of income before you become disabled. You can expect anywhere from 50 to 80 percent of your predisability income from all sources combined. Higher-paid workers tend to receive a benefit equal to a smaller percentage of their former pay than do lower-paid workers. If you pay your own premiums on a disability insurance policy, they will cost less if you accept a benefit equal to a smaller percentage of your predisability pay. You can also add a cost-of-living-adjustment clause to your policy for an extra premium. This clause would raise your disability payments based on an index tied to the yearly change in the Consumer Price Index (CPI).

Benefit payment method. Some policies call for weekly checks, but most pay monthly. A policy also might include a provision allowing the insurance company to pay the entire benefit in one lump sum, cutting short any further liability. If you think you can't manage to successfully allocate the money from a lump sum, you may want to avoid this type of insurance.

Beginning payment date. Some policies begin paying benefits within a month of your disability; most wait six months or even a year. The longer you can go without receiving insurance benefits, the lower your premiums will be. Before you choose a longer waiting period, however, make sure you have enough savings and other resources to cover your expenses over that time.

Payment caps. All policies limit the monthly amount of disability benefits paid to recipients. It could be as much as $5,000 or $6,000 or far less, depending on the policy. Try to estimate realistically how much income you would need if you were disabled.

Ending payment date. Disability insurance is designed to replace earned income, so benefits may last from one year to the rest of your life, depending on when you become ill or injured and what other sources of income are available to you. If you agree to receive benefits for a shorter time, your premiums will be lower. Most people buy policies that pay benefits until age 65 when they qualify for various government programs.

Renewability. The last thing you want to happen if you are disabled is for your insurance company to cancel your policy. Make sure that the coverage you buy is guaranteed non-cancelable, which means that it is renewable at the original premium price. If your insurance carrier does not offer a non-cancelable policy, it may offer a guaranteed renewable policy instead, which guarantees that your policy will be renewed no matter what your health condition, though the premium may change.

Additional Tolls: Tax Implications and Costs of Disability Insurance

If you become disabled and you have paid the premiums for disability insurance, any benefits you receive are free of federal, state, and local income taxes. However, if your employer has paid some or all of the premiums, your benefits are partially or totally taxable to you as ordinary income. Though prices vary widely among disability policies, depending on your age and occupation, you might expect to pay about $1,000 a year for $12,000 worth of annual disability income coverage.

Although several types of insurance companies offer disability coverage, life insurers specialize in the product and tend to offer the best options at the lowest prices. You most likely will obtain a much better price for more generous benefits if you buy through a group plan. However, if you cannot purchase coverage through your employer, union, or trade association or you need additional coverage, it often makes sense to purchase a supplemental individual policy.

A specialized type of disability insurance is tied to your ability to repay loans. Banks, finance companies, car dealerships, and other lenders sell *credit disability insurance,* which covers your loan payments if you become disabled. Mortgage lenders push mortgage *disability insurance,* which makes your home payments if you become disabled. In general, both credit and mortgage disability insurance policies are not good investments because they are overpriced. You are better served by more comprehensive forms of disability coverage.

The worksheet in Tollbooth 4.3 will help you total your potential sources of disability income. Fill in the monthly amount you would receive from each policy, the waiting period before benefits begin, and the number of years you would receive benefits. Although you may not want to even think about your possible need for disability income, it will be better for you in the long term. By completing this disability income worksheet when you are *not* disabled, you will have a better idea of how you might cope if such a tragedy ever occurred. By adding your potential sources of disability income, you can also calculate how much private insurance you need to buy.

Tollbooth 4.3

Disability Income Worksheet

Disability Insurance Program	Monthly $ Amount	Waiting Period (Months)	Benefits for How Long (Years)
Government Programs			
Black Lung	$		
Civil Service			
Department of Veterans Affairs			
Medicaid			
Social Security			
Workers' Compensation			
Group Programs			
Employer			
Sick Leave			
Union			
Individual Programs			
Auto			
Credit Disability			
Individual Disability			
Mortgage Disability			
Other (while disabled)			
Savings and Investments			
Other			
TOTAL MONTHLY INCOME (while disabled)	$		

▶ Pit Stop #4: Update Your Homeowners Insurance

Widows and widowers who are homeowners should carry adequate *homeowners insurance*. Doing so will probably mean continuing with your existing policy. The first thing you should do is simply make sure that *your* name —not that of your deceased spouse—is on the policy.

Detour: Protect Your Home Against Property Damage

The primary reason that you buy homeowners insurance is to compensate yourself for property damage or loss—and you certainly don't need any more loss in your life right now.

There are two sources of damage: natural occurrences and man- or equipment-made disasters. Some of the more common natural causes include earthquakes, fire, floods, hurricanes, mudslides, storms, tornadoes, volcanoes, wind, hail, and weight of snow. Losses caused by people or the malfunctioning of equipment include arson, burglary, electrical fires, explosions, riots, theft, vandalism, and water pipe breaks.

Insurers offer two types of policies to cover these risks:

1. *Named peril coverage,* which protects you against only the specific dangers spelled out in the insurance contract. The perils usually named are fire, wind, hail, riots, smoke, vandalism, and theft, among others. Under this policy, if you have a claim, you must show that the loss or damage was caused by one of the named perils.

2. *All-risk insurance,* which covers almost every possible source of loss or damage *except* those specifically named, such as floods, earthquake, nuclear war, dry rot, termites and insect damage, and wear and tear. You will need special insurance —for example, from the National Flood Insurance program—to cover those risks. Because the all-risk policy is more comprehensive, its premiums are usually higher than those on a named peril policy covering the same property.

There are six basic types of homeowner's policies, each offering protection against certain losses on both your home's structure and its contents. They are all labeled HO (which stands for *homeowners*), followed by a number. The most basic plan is HO-2. The most comprehensive plan, HO-3, is an all-risk policy that also provides special coverages. Policies for renters are labeled HO-4 and for condominium owners, HO-6. If you own an older home, you will need an HO-8 policy. Roadmap 4.2 shows the basics of what some of these plans cover.

The purpose of homeowners insurance is to replace what has been lost or damaged; therefore, in determining how much coverage to buy, follow the most important rule of homeowners insurance: *Buy enough to* replace *most or all of your property at risk.* Frequently, homeowners insure their homes and the contents of their homes for what they paid for them, perhaps years ago. When these homeowners suffer a loss, they find—to their dismay—that they are reimbursed only for the present market value of the objects, which is usually far less than it costs to replace them. Unless your homeowner's policy specifically stipulates that it pays replacement cost, the insurer covers only the actual, depreciated value of the goods. Although you will pay premiums that are 10 or 20 percent higher for replacement cost insurance, the coverage is worth the extra money.

If you cannot afford the premiums on full replacement cost insurance, the least you should settle for is 80 percent replacement cost. Cutting back from 100 percent to 80 percent will slash your premiums by as much as a quarter. However, if you settle for less than 80 percent, you expose yourself to too much financial risk. This is very dangerous, so if at all possible, purchase full replacement coverage! Whether you opt for 100 percent or the 80 percent, though, always insist on a clause that indexes your coverage to changes in inflation.

In addition to your regular homeowner's coverage, you might want to purchase special insurance, known as a *rider* or a *floater,* for particularly valuable artwork, collectibles, silver, furs, jewelry, or other items. Without these riders, you would collect nowhere near their true value if such precious objects were damaged or stolen.

Hazard: Don't Forget to Insure Your Home-Based Business

If you run a home-based business, or are thinking of doing so, you probably need extra insurance protection for all your equipment. Most homeowner's policies provide only $2,500 in coverage for property used for business purposes. Therefore, acquire an endorsement, or an additional clause that specifies particular items, to cover your computers, fax machines, office furniture, copiers, file cabinets, and other equipment.

Roadmap 4.2

Comparison of Coverage Under Selected Types of Homeowners Insurance Plans

HO-2 (the basic plan) & HO-8 (for older homes)

Both the HO-2 policy (the basic plan) and the HO-8 policy (for older homes) protect against the following specific perils:

1. Fire or lightning
2. Windstorm or hail
3. Explosion
4. Riot or civil disturbance
5. Damage from an aircraft
6. Damage from a vehicle
7. Smoke damage
8. Vandalism or malicious mischief
9. Theft
10. Breakage of glass that is part of a building
11. Volcanic eruption

HO-2 (the broad coverage plan)

The HO-2, or broad coverage, policy covers all of the perils of an HO-1, as well as the following:

▶ Falling object
▶ Weight of ice, snow, or sleet
▶ Freezing of a plumbing, a heating, or an air-conditioning system, of an automatic fire protective sprinkler system, or of a household appliance
▶ Accidental discharge or overflow of water or steam from a plumbing, a heating, or an air-conditioning system
▶ Sudden and accidental discharge from an artificially generated electric current
▶ Sudden and accidental tearing apart, cracking, burning, or bulging of a heating, an air-conditioning, or a protective sprinkler system, or an appliance for heating water

HO-4 (for renters) & HO-6 (for condo owners)

The HO-4 for renters and the HO-6 for condo owners cover the same perils as the HO-2 (see above). In addition, these policies cover contents and some structural aspects of an apartment or condominium, such as a wall that is not shared with another unit or separate balcony.

Many insurance companies offer special-rate policies tailored to cover small businesses. Usually, homeowner's policies do not cover liabilities arising out of business activities. For example, you would not be covered against a suit filed by a delivery person who falls on your property while delivering a package for your business. A *small business specialty policy* insures against such an event. You might also investigate *business interruption insurance,* which pays for your temporary relocation to other quarters while your office is being repaired due to fire or another disaster.

Alternate Route: Homeowners Insurance for Renters and Condo Owners

If you rent, your landlord's insurance covers the building in which you live, but you should still buy a separate policy to cover your possessions. The provisions of a renter's policy are nearly identical to those of homeowner's coverage. You are protected against loss or damage from the most common perils (again, such as fire, explosion, water damage, vandalism, or theft). If you own valuables, such as jewelry or computers, you probably need a floater to provide coverage beyond the typical limits. Most renters' policies impose a $1,000 limit on jewelry, $3,000 to $10,000 on computers, and $2,500 to $10,000 on silverware. As with homeowners insurance, *it is best to buy replacement cost coverage rather than a policy based on cash value.*

Insurance for condominium owners is similar to coverage available for renters. The condominium association buys insurance that protects the buildings, grounds, and common areas, but each owner must obtain special condominium coverage for the contents of their apartments, walls that are not shared with other apartments, and other things that are not commonly owned, as well as liability claims.

Assessing the Toll: Take Inventory of Your Household Goods

Keeping those general guidelines in mind, determine how much homeowners insurance you need. If you haven't done this before, you should first take a household inventory to see what actually needs insuring. If you have done this before, you may want to update it if you've sold or given away items that belonged to your late spouse, or your policy may not cover valuables that you have acquired recently. An easy way to tote up the worth of your possessions is to take a household inventory using a household inventory worksheet, shown in Tollbooth 4.4.

Walk around your home and list on an inventory sheet each item you own, what you paid for it, and how much it might cost to replace. Also note model and serial numbers. If you have no idea what things cost today, you might consider bringing in an appraiser to help you.

In addition to listing your household possessions, photograph or videotape each room. If you videotape, talk about the objects you are taping and estimate how much they cost. Keep the pictures or tape somewhere other than your home, such as at work, so you will have access to it if your house is destroyed or damaged. These physical records can be invaluable if you ever must file a claim and convince an adjuster that you owned a particular item or what an item is worth. Keep in mind that you want to make your life easier, in case something does happen to your home and you need your homeowner's insurance money.

Extra Air Bags: Liability Coverage

In addition to reimbursing you for lost or damaged property, homeowners insurance protects you and insured members of your household against claims and lawsuits for injuries or property damage that you or your family members may have caused accidentally.

For example, if your son throws a baseball through your neighbor's window, your neighbor can sue you to pay for the damage. If your dog bites the mail carrier, your liability insurance would cover their medical expenses. Someone who slips on ice on your sidewalk may also sue you for negligence. This general liability coverage does not apply to any damage you do in your car, which is covered by your auto liability insurance.

If you think the chances of being sued are remote, think again. To protect yourself, purchase extra liability coverage as part of your regular policy.

Tollbooth 4.4

Household Inventory Worksheet

Article and Description	Purchase Price	Replacement Cost	Total Purchase Cost	Total Replacement Cost
Bathrooms				
Carpets/Rugs	$_____	$_____		
Clothes Hampers	_____	_____		
Curtains	_____	_____		
Dressing Tables	_____	_____		
Electrical Appliances	_____	_____		
Lighting Fixtures	_____	_____		
Linens	_____	_____		
Scales	_____	_____		
Shower Curtains	_____	_____		
Other	_____	_____		
Total for Bathrooms			$_____	$_____
Bedrooms				
Beds/Mattresses	$_____	$_____		
Books/Bookcases	_____	_____		
Carpets/Rugs	_____	_____		
Chairs	_____	_____		
Clocks	_____	_____		
Clothing	_____	_____		
Curtains/Drapes	_____	_____		
Desks	_____	_____		
Dressers	_____	_____		
Lamps	_____	_____		
Mirrors	_____	_____		
Plants	_____	_____		
Records/Tapes/CDs	_____	_____		
Stereos/Radios	_____	_____		
Tables	_____	_____		
Televisions	_____	_____		
Wall Hangings/Pictures	_____	_____		
Wall Units	_____	_____		
Other	_____	_____		
Total for Bedrooms			$_____	$_____
Dining Room				
Buffets	$_____	$_____		
Carpets/Rugs	_____	_____		
Chairs	_____	_____		

Article and Description	Purchase Price	Replacement Cost	Total Purchase Cost	Total Replacement Cost
Dining Room (cont'd)				
China	_____	_____		
Clocks	_____	_____		
Curtains/Drapes	_____	_____		
Glassware	_____	_____		
Lamps/Fixtures	_____	_____		
Silverware	_____	_____		
Tables	_____	_____		
Wall Hangings/Pictures	_____	_____		
Other	_____	_____		
Total for Dining Room			$_____	$_____
Garage/Basement/Attic				
Furniture	$_____	$_____		
Ladders	_____	_____		
Lawn Mowers	_____	_____		
Luggage	_____	_____		
Shovels	_____	_____		
Snowblowers	_____	_____		
Sports Equipment	_____	_____		
Sprinklers/Hoses	_____	_____		
Tools/Supplies	_____	_____		
Toys	_____	_____		
Washer/Dryer	_____	_____		
Wheelbarrows	_____	_____		
Work Benches	_____	_____		
Other	_____	_____		
Total for Garage/ Basement/Attic			$_____	$_____
Kitchen				
Buffets	$_____	$_____		
Cabinets	_____	_____		
Chairs	_____	_____		
Clocks	_____	_____		
Curtains	_____	_____		
Dishes	_____	_____		
Dishwasher	_____	_____		
Disposal/Trash Compactor	_____	_____		
Food/Supplies	_____	_____		
Freezer	_____	_____		
Glassware	_____	_____		
Lighting Fixtures	_____	_____		
Refrigerator	_____	_____		

Article and Description	Purchase Price	Replacement Cost	Total Purchase Cost	Total Replacement Cost
Kitchen (cont'd)				
Pots/Pans	_____	_____		
Radio/Television	_____	_____		
Small Appliances	_____	_____		
Stove	_____	_____		
Tables	_____	_____		
Washer/Dryer	_____	_____		
Other	_____	_____		
Total for Kitchen			$_____	$_____
Living Room				
Books/Bookcases	$_____	$_____		
Carpets/Rugs	_____	_____		
Chairs	_____	_____		
Clocks	_____	_____		
Curtains/Drapes	_____	_____		
Desks	_____	_____		
Lamps	_____	_____		
Mirrors	_____	_____		
Musical Instruments	_____	_____		
Plants	_____	_____		
Records/Tapes/CDs	_____	_____		
Sofas	_____	_____		
Stereo/Radio	_____	_____		
Tables	_____	_____		
Television	_____	_____		
Wall Hangings/Pictures	_____	_____		
Wall Units	_____	_____		
Other	_____	_____		
Total for Living Room			$_____	$_____
Porch/Patio				
Carpets/Rugs	$_____	$_____		
Chairs	_____	_____		
Lamps	_____	_____		
Outdoor Cooking Equipment	_____	_____		
Outdoor Furniture	_____	_____		
Plants/Planters	_____	_____		
Tables	_____	_____		
Other	_____	_____		
Total for Porch/Patio			$_____	$_____
TOTAL HOUSEHOLD			$_____	$_____

This is generally known as *umbrella coverage,* and it usually extends your liability insurance to $1 million or more.

Reducing Your Tolls: Minimizing Your Premium for Homeowners Insurance

The best way to qualify for the lowest insurance rates is to guard against accidents, thefts, and losses. Some of the more obvious precautions you can take, which often qualify for direct discounts, include the following:

► Install deadbolt locks on doors and key locks on windows. If your home or apartment is at street level, add grates or grilles to protect windows.

► Install a burglar alarm system that attaches to doors and windows, that rings loudly if activated, and that automatically notifies the local police department or alarm company of an intruder.

► Keep wiring in top condition.

► Maintain stairs, railings, carpets, and flooring to minimize the possibility of slips or falls.

► Keep fresh batteries in smoke detectors, and install a sprinkler system and fire alarm that automatically alerts the fire department when it senses smoke.

► Install exterior lights to make it difficult for a burglar to work in secrecy.

► Stop smoking cigarettes because nonsmokers are less likely to start fires than smokers.

Most companies also shave your premiums if you are a long-time customer who has never filed a claim or if you have policies for auto or life insurance with the same company.

Rates on homeowner's policies are also based on the neighborhood in which your home is located. Obviously, owners of homes in crime-infested areas will pay higher premiums than those whose neighborhoods boast tight security and few crimes. Also, the closer your home is to fire and police protection, the lower your premiums. In general, newer homes qualify for lower rates than older homes because more can go wrong in older buildings as wiring, plumbing, and heating systems deteriorate over time.

Another way to cut your premiums is to accept higher deductibles. If you increase the amount of loss you cover out of your own pocket from $250 to $1,000 or more, your premium cost plummets. Even when you agree to a substantial deductible, however, you gain protection against the enormous losses that homeowners insurance is designed to cover.

▶ Pit Stop #5: Update Your Auto Insurance

As long as you own a car, you must have auto insurance. If you lost your spouse, make sure that the auto insurance policy is in your name, not your spouse's. If the policy was purchased in your spouse's name, transfer it to yours. You will need to maintain the standard auto insurance coverages—comprehensive, liability, uninsured motorist, and collision. If you own an old car of little value, reduce the comprehensive and collision coverage. To cut your premium costs, qualify for as many discounts as possible. Some of the most common discounts are given for installing antitheft devices and passive restraints like air bags and automatic seat belts; passing a driver education course; and promising to drive fewer than a specific number of miles each year, as set by the insurance company. Many insurers also offer discounts to those older than age 50 who have good driving records.

Kick the Tires: Make Sure You Get the Car Insurance You Need

If your spouse handled your car insurance and you're unfamiliar with the terminology, the following paragraphs offer a brief explanation of the primary factors you need to consider when buying car insurance coverage.

Bodily injury. If you hit someone with your car and cause injury or death because you were driving negligently, you must pay for the damages caused by the accident. These damages include the medical bills and lost wages of the person you injured. The person can also sue for pain and suffering if you live in a state that assesses fault for accidents.

Property damage. This liability insurance covers any damage that you cause to another person's property by driving negligently. This may include damage to another car or other property, such as a fence or a tree. Because it is usually less expensive to damage property than to injure people, property liability is cheaper and generally purchased in smaller amounts.

Collision. One of the main reasons you buy auto insurance is to reimburse you if your car is seriously damaged in a collision. Your policy will pay you to fix the car and bring it back to its condition before the accident. Most policies will pay your repair bills in full, less the deductible. If the repairs total $3,000, for example, you receive a check for $3,000. Some policies, however, reimburse you only for the *book value* of the damaged property. In this case, the insurance company would rather pay you what the car was worth before the accident (assuming plenty of depreciation), knowing that this amount could not bring it back to a usable condition. No insurance settlement pays enough for a new car. Therefore, try to obtain a policy that reimburses you for replacement cost, not the book value.

The older and less valuable your car becomes, the less comprehensive and collision coverage you need. You can also cut your collision premiums by raising your deductible as the car ages. You might start with $500 and increase it to $1,000 or more after two or three years of ownership. Once your car's value drops to about $1,000, it probably makes sense to drop collision and comprehensive coverage because what you might collect from a claim will not replace the car anyway.

Comprehensive. This coverage pays for losses sustained by your car other than in collisions with cars or property. Comprehensive coverage includes such things as fire, theft, storm damage, falling objects, explosions, earthquakes, floods, riots, and collisions with birds and other animals. For example, if a thief breaks your window and takes your car stereo, you would file a claim under the comprehensive portion of your policy. As with collision insurance, the less valuable your car becomes over time, the less comprehensive coverage you need. You can also save money by raising your deductible from about $500 to $1,000 or more.

Medical payments. Medical coverage, known as *med pay,* pays doctor and hospital bills—as well as funeral expenses, if needed—brought about by injuries that you and your passengers sustain in a car accident. Med pay also kicks in if you or a family member is hit by a car when walking as a pedestrian or if you or a family member is hurt when riding in someone else's car. Medical bills are covered up to the limit specified in the policy, regardless of who causes the accident. Most policies limit coverage for each injured individual in a car, up to as much as $5,000 apiece. For example, if three people are in your car when you have an accident, the insurer may have to pay as much as $15,000 in medical bills.

Some people skimp on med pay coverage because they figure that their bills will be covered by their health insurance. Economizing on such coverage, however, is usually not a good idea for two reasons. First, while your health insurance may be topnotch, your passengers may not have good coverage. (If you don't have good health insurance coverage, med pay is even more important.) Second, med pay covers funeral expenses, which are not reimbursed by health insurance. For the relatively small med pay premium, the extra coverage is worthwhile. In some states, med pay is not optional, so you don't have a choice over whether to carry it or not.

Personal injury. In states with no-fault insurance laws, personal injury protection (PIP) covers a broader assortment of medical charges than med pay does. In addition to covering doctor's bills, PIP also replaces lost wages or pays to replace the services of someone injured in a car accident. For example, if you are a stay-at-home parent who is laid up because of an auto accident, PIP payments would cover baby-sitter fees until you can care for your children again. PIP is often required in states with no-fault plans though it is also usually available in states assessing fault. It is relatively inexpensive and usually worth adding to your policy.

Uninsured or underinsured motorist. This coverage protects you if you are involved in an accident with a driver who is either totally uninsured or severely underinsured. It also protects you if you are injured by a hit-and-run driver. With auto insurance premiums skyrocketing these days, some people drive around with little or no coverage. If such an uninsured or underinsured driver causes an accident, your uninsured motorist coverage pays you what you would be entitled to if the other driver had full insurance. You can collect not only for medical bills caused by the accident but also for lost wages and pain and suffering. Uninsured or underinsured motorist coverage is very inexpensive because the odds of being in an accident with an under- or uninsured driver are relatively small. Even if the insurance is optional in your state, obtain it to protect yourself.

Stay on Course: Choosing a Car Insurance Company

Before you renew your insurance, assess each of these insurance components carefully to determine what insurance you need and how much you can afford. Also, keep in mind that by accepting higher deductibles and lower coverage limits, you can reduce your premium. But don't limit your coverage or raise your deductibles so much that the policy won't protect you when you really need it!

The auto insurance business is extremely competitive, so it pays to shop around. Get a quote from a captive agent who works for a large insurer like Allstate, State Farm, or Geico, and compare it to the best price that you obtain from an independent agent who represents several companies.

The price you are quoted for auto coverage depends not only on the insurer's rates but also on your driving record, where you live, and the kind of car you wish to insure. Your gender and marital status also affect your premium because women and married people are statistically less likely to have accidents than men and singles. Your price will be quite low if you have never had an accident, live in a quiet suburb, and drive a modest sedan. On the other hand, expect to pay a high premium if you have a history of claims, you live in a high-crime area, and you own a sports car or luxury sedan. Many companies will not even insure certain cars at any price.

Before you commit to a company, check its claim procedure. Make sure the firm has claims adjusters near your home who can examine your car, assess the damage, and process your claim quickly and efficiently. Also inquire whether your rates will soar or the company will drop you altogether if you file a claim. Some companies take such a drastic step after only one claim —even if the accident was not your fault. It is better to work with a company that's a bit more understanding.

If, for whatever reason, you are not able to find a commercial insurance company that will issue you a policy at a reasonable cost or that will issue a policy at all, you may have to obtain a state-sponsored insurance plan. Unfortunately, because these plans must accept everyone—no matter what the risk—their premiums are far higher than those under commercial policies. Your state's plan might be called a *joint underwriting association* (JUA) or an *assigned-risk plan*. But whatever its name, it is far less preferable than qualifying for coverage with a private insurance company.

▶ Last Stop

Now that you know more about all types of insurance that you need, you can make some informed decisions. Start with updating your own life insurance, so your survivors and beneficiaries will be well cared for. Calculate what you think they'll need, then choose from the four basic types of coverage (term, whole life, universal life, and variable life): decide what's best for you based on how much coverage you need, how much premium you can afford, and whether you want insurance only for its death benefit or also for its savings potential.

In addition, make sure you update your health insurance, whether you choose a traditional plan, an HMO, a PPO, Medicare, or a specialized health insurance plan. Then update your disability insurance, because you need to be protected in case you become seriously injured or ill and can't work. Don't forget your homeowners insurance (whether you rent or own), to protect your home from natural disasters or theft, and your car insurance. These may seem mundane, but they're important, too.

Check Your Map
Routes to Investing Well

So far this book has focused primarily on helping you *update* all critical financial information: to get organized in terms of recordkeeping and bill paying, creating a new budget for this next phase of your life; to update your will and estate plans so that your beneficiaries are protected; to make sure you're thinking about your retirement and future financial needs; and to ensure that you're insured. Once you've taken care of those more pressing, immediate concerns, you should start to think a little further down the road; you need to look at long-term plans.

Therefore, this chapter takes a longer-range view of your investments for the future. It covers all areas you might consider: cash, bonds, stocks, mutual funds, and real estate. Of course, entire books are written on each of these subjects, but this chapter gives you an overview to help you invest for yourself or simply discuss your portfolio intelligently with your broker or financial advisor.

▶ Map a New Route: Reassess Your Financial Goals And Tolerance For Risk

Before we get into the nitty-gritty, you should first prioritize your financial goals. Now that you are alone, you may have different priorities. For instance, you might want to move to another home. You should also reassess your risk tolerance before you reallocate your investment portfolio. You might find that you're more willing to take risk than your spouse was, or perhaps you are more conservative. Whatever the case, know where you stand on the risk spectrum before you make any investment moves.

How Fast Are You Willing to Go? Determining Your Tolerance for Risk

Risk tolerance is how you feel and react when the value of your investments declines. For example, if you had allocated 70 percent of your portfolio to stocks and regularly added to your account, then in 2004, you would have watched the bear market take 30 percent of your stocks' value. Can you continue to invest the new dollars needed to maintain your 70 percent allocation to equities, while at the same time watching the value of your portfolio go down?

Over longer periods of time (i.e., 10 to 20 years), history has shown that stocks outperform all other asset classes, so a well-thought-out investment plan can help you stay the course during the market's ups and downs. You want to avoid making emotionally based decisions that will hurt your portfolio's performance over the long run. Roadmap 5.1 offers a guideline to help you determine the right percentage of equity exposure for you based on your risk tolerance.

Next, you should factor in the percentage of loss you personally find tolerable with the investment time horizon that you're expecting; see Roadmap 5.2: the lower of the two percentages should be your portfolio's equity allocation. Defining your personal level of risk tolerance allows you to build a portfolio most suited to helping you reach your future financial goals while allowing you to invest within your comfort zone.

Finally, Roadmap 5.3 is a short questionnaire that may offer some insight into your personal feelings toward risk. It will also rank some of the common factors that determine your ability to take on risk. These factors include age, income, current savings, and general investment knowledge.

Roadmap 5.1

How Much to Invest in Equities Depending on Your Risk Tolerance

Maximum Tolerable Loss	Maximum Equity Exposure
5%	20%
10	30
15	40
20	50
25	60
30	70
35	80
40	90
50	100

You should use the questions in Roadmap 5.3 and your score as a guide only, because your actual investment plan may vary based on additional information not covered in the questionnaire. But after you have scored your risk tolerance, the next step is creating a portfolio of investments that matches your tolerance for risk.

As you see from the scoring of the questionnaire, you'll find yourself in one of five categories. The asset allocations suggested for each category offer hypothetical examples of the types of allocations available. Your circumstances may change, so you should review your investment allocation periodically and adjust as needed. The investments you select will determine the overall aggressiveness and volatility of your portfolio. Remember that the value of your portfolio will fluctuate with market conditions.

1. *Ultraconservative.* As an ultraconservative investor, you prefer income-oriented, guaranteed investments such as CDs and bonds. Your need for income is high and your tolerance for risk is very low.

2. *Fairly Conservative.* As a fairly conservative investor, you are still uncomfortable with the volatility inherent in the stock market. However,

Roadmap 5.2

Determining How Much to Invest in Equities

Time Horizon	Maximum Allocation in Equities
0-3 years	0%
4-5 years	20
6 years	30
7 years	40
8 years	50
9 years	60
10 years	70
11+ years	80

you realize that a long-term commitment to quality growth investments should help you reach your financial goals. Therefore, although you're still primarily interested in fixed income-producing assets, you are willing to increase your allocation to balanced funds and some growth and income funds. If you venture into individual stocks, you are more likely to lean toward large cap, dividend-paying companies.

3. *Moderate.* Moderate investors see themselves as the tortoise in "The Tortoise and the Hare." You are definitely interested in achieving reasonable returns and you have attempted to measure and quantify the risk. You realize there will be periods of negative returns, yet you are determined to commit to a long-term strategy of investing in a variety of growth investments that include large cap stocks, midcap stocks, and even international stocks. However, to reduce the overall volatility of your portfolio, you'll have a healthy portion held in fixed-income assets.

4. *Fairly Aggressive.* As a fairly aggressive investor, you'll be critically aware of the risk-return ratio between your various investment options. You

Roadmap 5.3

Measuring Your Risk Tolerance

Please circle the number preceding each of your answers.

What is your age?

1 65 and over
3 36-64
5 35 and under

What is your time horizon for investing this money?

1 1 year
2 2-5 years
3 5-10 years
4 10-20 years
5 20 years or longer

What is your primary objective for this money?

1 Safety of principal
2 Current income
3 Growth and income
4 Conservative growth
5 Aggressive growth

Regarding your income, do you expect it to:

1 Decrease dramatically in the future?
2 Decrease a slight amount in the future?
3 Stay about the same?
4 Increase with the pace of inflation?
5 Increase dramatically?

What amount of money do you have set aside for emergencies?

1 None
3 Enough to cover three months of expenses
5 Enough to cover six or more months of expenses

Which statement best describes your personal investment experience?

1 I have never been responsible for investing any money.
2 I am a relatively new investor.
3 I have invested some of my money through IRAs and through
   employer-sponsored retirement plans (401(k)s) for quite some time,
   but now I am ready to develop additional investment strategies.

4 I have invested for quite some time and am fairly confident in my ability to make prudent investment decisions.

5 I have invested money for years and have a definite knowledge of how the various stock and bond markets work.

Regarding your view of risk, which investment would you be more comfortable making?

1 I am comfortable investing in savings accounts and CDs (certificates of deposit) that are FDIC insured.

2 I invest in savings accounts and CDs, but I also own various income-producing bonds and/or bond mutual funds.

3 I have invested in a broad array of stocks, bonds, and mutual funds, but only those of the highest quality.

4 I have invested primarily in growth stocks and growth stock mutual funds.

5 I like to pick out new and emerging growth companies and aggressive growth stock mutual funds.

To understand your risk tolerance more clearly, which investment would you be more likely to invest in?

1 This investment has a 20-year average annual return of 6 percent. It has achieved those returns with infrequent and very slight downturns. This investment has never experienced a negative return.

3 This investment has a 20-year average annual return of 9 percent. It has achieved those returns with a few moderate downturns when the decline lasted less than six months and then began to recover. It has experienced more than one year of negative returns.

5 This investment has a 20-year average annual return of 14 percent. It has achieved those returns while cycling through several periods of above-average returns and several periods of substantially negative returns.

To score the risk tolerance test, simply add up the points. You receive one point for each number that you circled. For example, if you circled a 1, you receive 1 point. If you circled a 4, you receive 4 points. The lowest number of points is 8 and the highest number is 40. Please count the number of points you circled and place a star on the risk tolerance scale below:

Ultra-conservative	Fairly Conservative	Moderate	Fairly Aggressive	Ultra-aggressive
8 10 12 14	16 18 20	22 24 26	28 30 32 34	36 38 40

are not at all interested in income, so you spread your money among a variety of more aggressive growth stocks and growth mutual funds. You would be interested in diversifying your money into all the major growth categories (large cap, midcap, small cap, and international). You would want to structure your portfolio to take advantage of growth stock cycles and value stock cycles by owning both types. And because of the higher level of volatility, you'd want to be sure you set a consistent schedule to monitor your progress.

5. *Ultra-aggressive.* As an ultra-aggressive investor, you're interested in high return. You are aware of the risks, but you believe in making the most of every dollar. You are interested in investing in growth sectors. You look to new industries for your excitement. However, you are not carried away. You place a considerable portion of your portfolio into large cap and midcap growth stocks. You realize the importance of diversification and know there will be wild swings in the month-to-month value of your accounts.

Plan Multiple Routes: Diversify!

To reduce your investing risk, diversify the actual markets in which you are investing your money. As described, begin by deciding what percentage of your assets you want in cash, in bonds, and in stocks. You can also add more asset classes like real estate and precious metals; the most sophisticated investors also look at other commodities and financial futures contracts (often called managed futures). You can thus reduce market risk by diversifying the asset classes in which you invest your money.

You can also reduce some market risk through sector rotation. Though markets often fall in unison, there are usually one or two sectors of the market that do well when other sectors are performing poorly. The stock market can be categorized into the following sectors:

- ► Basic materials
- ► Energy
- ► Technology
- ► Health care
- ► Consumer cyclicals (Durable)
- ► Consumer cyclicals (Nondurable)
- ► Consumer noncyclicals
- ► Utilities

▶ Financials
▶ Transportation
▶ Telecommunications

You might see a steep decline in basic materials or energy while such sectors as heath care or technology are rebounding.

How Many Miles to the Gallon? Determining Your Financial Objectives

Finally, what are your financial objectives, and how much potential risk will you likely need to take on to reach them? Sometimes, the amount of money you need drives the amount of risk or equity exposure you will take on. For example, if, based on the number of years to retirement, you need an 8 percent return on your investment, roughly 60 percent of your portfolio should be allocated to equities. But would you still be able to sleep at night while taking this kind of risk with your money?

If the risk to achieve the return is more than you can stomach, but you don't want to reduce your retirement spending plan, the options are to increase your savings or delay your expected retirement date (or some combination of the two) to make up for the lower expected return that comes with taking less risk. The other alternative would be to accept a reduced retirement income. Whatever route you choose, if you develop a good game plan and stick with it, you have the potential to be rewarded.

Depending on your age and the amount of assets you have, you will probably want to invest conservatively and emphasize *income* over growth of *capital.* The largest amount of money you will have to invest will most likely come from your spouse's life insurance policy (assuming you had bought insurance coverage). Because this capital is designed to replace your spouse's income, you should invest it in *income-producing securities,* such as utility stocks; Treasury, municipal, or corporate bonds; or mutual funds holding such stocks and bonds. Stock mutual funds that are conservative and produce a steady stream of income include equity income, growth and income, convertible, balanced, and flexible funds. All bond funds (except zero-coupon funds) pay regular income, though you will probably want to concentrate on government, corporate, municipal, and international bond funds.

Here's a word of caution: Do not invest *all* your inherited capital in income-oriented funds. Assuming that you will live a long time, you should have some percentage—perhaps as much as 50 percent or more—of your portfolio in *growth-oriented* stocks and stock mutual funds. As the value of such funds increases over time, your assets will be protected against inflation.

Of course, you will need an emergency cash reserve to pay bills and meet unexpected expenses. This might amount to 5 to 10 percent of the value of your portfolio. As you calculate the optimal allocation of your assets among stocks, bonds, and cash, keep your risk tolerance in mind. Do not take substantial risks if doing so makes you uncomfortable. On the other hand, don't invest your money *so* conservatively that it doesn't grow fast enough to keep up with inflation or your expenses.

So let's look at the six basic roads to long-term investing, beginning with the most basic: cash.

▶ Route #1: Count Your Cash Assets

Assuming your spouse did not have the assets in stocks, bonds, and other financial instruments, and if you are a beginner at investing, chances are that you have most of your money in cash instruments. By *cash,* we mean investments that are totally safe from loss of principal, including checking, savings, and certificate of deposit (CD) accounts at banks and savings and loans, money-market mutual funds, and Treasury bills (T-bills).

Cash instruments play an important stabilizing role in your investment portfolio. No matter how much or how little interest your cash earns, and although it may not keep pace with inflation, it cannot fall in principal value (which certainly cannot be said for stocks and bonds). Cash can therefore provide a haven when stock and bond prices are falling. Clearly, it is important to have cash available to meet everyday living expenses.

Many cash instruments, including money-market accounts, and passbook savings accounts are instantly accessible either through a check privilege or by withdrawing cash at an ATM. Other cash vehicles, including CDs and T-bills (which have short maturities) allow you to get at your money when the instruments mature in a few months. The liquidity of cash is one of its main benefits.

Even though you might think you will never have to worry about it, don't keep more than $100,000 in one account at a time. The federal insurance agencies (e.g., the FDIC) do not insure more than $100,000 per account, and they may or may not cover any amount over that if a bank is seized or liquidated.

When deciding how much money to allocate to different kinds of cash accounts, you should consider both convenience and yield. Because all of these alternatives are absolutely safe, they are all low risk. The following "stops" rundown the advantages and disadvantages of the different kinds of cash instruments, starting with the lowest yielding and ending with the highest yielding.

Stop #1: Passbook Savings Accounts and Money-Market Deposit Accounts

Passbook savings accounts used to be the most popular way to save, but they're not as popular as they used to be because interest rates have fallen from about 5 percent in the early 1980s to the 1 to 2 percent range. Therefore, unless you do not have enough money to meet minimum balance requirements on other higher yielding accounts, passbook savings plans are not very attractive investments. The fees a bank charges to maintain a passbook account may eat up a significant portion of your interest earnings unless you maintain a large enough balance.

Money-market deposit accounts (MMDAs) are the banking industry's answer to the money-market mutual fund (described in Stop #2). Banks can pay whatever they wish on MMDAs. Their rates will always be higher than those on passbook savings accounts, though not always much higher, and your access to an MMDA is somewhat restricted. According to federal banking law, you can write three checks of any amount and make three electronic transfers a month on your MMDA. Your best strategy is to make three large transfers a month into your checking account, for which you can write checks. This way, most of your money will be earning high interest for a longer period of time.

Like they do for other accounts, banks usually require a minimum balance of at least $1,000 to open an MMDA. Most banks also charge fees for keeping a low balance, though often they will pay higher interest if you keep more money in your account. If you want to consolidate most of your cash at a bank in one liquid account, the MMDA is the best place to do it. It will pay the highest yields of any readily accessible product the bank offers.

Stop #2: Money-Market Mutual Funds

Money-market mutual funds are *run by fund management companies,* who buy short-term securities that offer the best yields available in the market-place at any given time.

1. Money-market mutual funds are *not insured by the FDIC* or any other government agency; however, there has never been a default or even a near-default in a money-market mutual fund.
2. Money-market mutual funds come in both *taxable and tax-free varieties*; interest from bank MMDAs is *always taxable*.
3. Money-market mutual fund *yields are usually higher* than those paid by bank MMDAs.
4. Money-market mutual funds *are widely diversified*.
5. Money-market funds *are credited with interest daily,* and the interest is reinvested automatically in more fund shares. Money-market mutual funds assess *annual management fees* of less than 1 percent annually. This fee is subtracted before a yield is quoted to you.

Stop #3: Treasury Bills

T-bills, as they are called, provide the ultimate in safety and liquidity and are therefore among investors' favorite havens for cash. The minimum accepted for a T-bill purchase is $10,000. T-bills are backed by the full faith and credit of the U.S. government and normally mature in 13 or 26 weeks. As a rule, the longer you commit your money, the higher your yield will be; however, yields on T-bills tend to be *lower* than yields on money market mutual funds because of the extra security they offer. The supply of and demand for bills ultimately determine the average yield on each T-bill.

You can buy a T-bill directly from any Federal Reserve Bank or branch (see Appendix B for a list of these), by mail, or through the Treasury Direct program with no fee. Alternatively, you can buy a Treasury bill through any broker or bank for a minimal charge of about $25. (That fee, of course, reduces your effective yield.) Like the interest on all Treasury securities, your T-bill's interest is taxable for federal income tax purposes, but it is not taxable at the state or local level.

Stop #4: Certificates of Deposit (CDs)

CDs are bank, savings and loan, or credit union instruments that allow you to lock in an interest rate for a specific period of time. If you withdraw your money from the CD before the CD matures, you face an early-withdrawal penalty set by each bank—often three to six months' interest. The most popular CDs mature in three months, six months, and one year, although banks offer CDs with maturities as long as five years. Some banks even offer so-called designer CDs, for which you decide the maturity and the bank quotes you a yield. Generally, the longer you commit your money, the higher your CD's yield will be. Banks usually set some minimum amount for CDs, which can be as low as $100 or as much as $1,000, but they never charge a fee to buy a certificate.

All interest from CDs is taxable at the federal, state, and local levels in the year it is received, even if the interest is reinvested. Remember to calculate the effect of those taxes when you compare CD returns against other alternatives, like tax-free money funds or municipal bonds.

You do not have to restrict your search for high yields to your neighborhood or even your state. Many banks accept out-of-state deposits by wire or mail, and the highest yields around the country are publicized in major financial newspapers, magazines, newsletters, and Web sites (see Appendix B for suggestions).

You can also buy CDs indirectly from brokerage firms, most of which sell CDs from banks across the country, which lets you buy a CD that is probably yielding more than your local bank's. You are still protected by federal deposit insurance, as long as you invest less than $100,000 (which you should!). There is no fee to you because the bank pays a fee to the broker to solicit clients.

▶ Route #2: Find Your Fixed-Income Assets: Bonds

When you invest in a *bond,* you are loaning the issuer of that bond your money in return for a fixed rate of interest and a promise to repay the "loan" at a specific date in the future. Normally, you receive interest payments every six months, and when the bond matures, you receive your original principal, no matter how much the price of the bond fluctuated since you bought it. Bonds allow you to lock in a set rate of income for a long period of time, which can give your financial plan a rock-solid foundation.

Paying the Toll: How Bonds Are Priced

Bonds are normally quoted on a price scale of 0 to 200, with 100 being the price at which the bond was issued, or what is known as *par*. Bonds are sold in denominations of $1,000, so a price of 100 means that the bond is trading at $1,000 per bond or 100 percent of the issue price. If the bond's price rises to 110, your holding is now worth $1,100. Most bond dealers like to deal in larger denominations, so keep in mind that smaller trades will subject you to larger dealer markups.

Unlike stock transactions, bond buy-and-sell transactions normally occur without a separate commission charge. Instead, a broker makes money from a transaction by taking a piece of the spread between the buying and selling prices. If you hold a bond until maturity there is no "sale" and therefore no additional cost. Because it is a competitive market, you should shop around among brokers to get the best deal.

When you consider investing in bonds, you should understand that *bond prices move in the opposite direction of interest rates*. You might think that rising interest rates would be good for your bond, but nothing could be further from the truth. Even though it sounds illogical, it is true that when interest rates rise, bond prices fall. When interest rates fall, bond prices rise. This is because bonds are a *fixed-rate* instrument, which means that the bond's rate is *locked in* at whatever level it was when the bond was first issued. The trading price of the bond becomes more or less valuable as interest rates fall or rise. (Barring unforeseen circumstances, if you keep the bond until it matures, you will receive the full par value.)

Falling bond prices can be an opportunity. If you buy a bond when its price is below par, your *effective rate* of interest is higher than it would be had you bought it at par. If, for example, a bond pays 10 percent at par, and you bought it for 90 (or $900), you would receive $100 in interest, but because you only invested $900, your effective rate is a bit over 11 percent. (Of course, the reverse is true as well.)

The longer the maturity of your bond, the more its price will react to the ups and downs of interest rates. A bond that locks in a high interest rate for 20 or 30 years is much more valuable to an investor if interest rates have fallen than a bond that matures in a year or two. Conversely, if interest rates have risen, the investor would rather get their money back quickly so that they can reinvest at higher rates. This bond volatility should always factor into your decision to buy bonds.

On the Road to Buying the Right Type of Bond for You

Now that you understand the basics of bonds, you should know the advantages and disadvantages of the several types of bonds that exist. Selecting the best bonds for you depends on the size of your assets, your financial goals, your time horizon, your risk tolerance, your tax situation, and your knowledge level. The following "stops" briefly describe each type of bond, starting with the most conservative (Treasuries) and ending with the most speculative (junk bonds), followed by bond funds.

Stop #1: Treasury Securities. Bonds issued by the U.S. government are considered the safest around because they are backed by the full faith and credit of the U.S. government, and therefore are free from the risk of default. Because of this, Treasuries are the benchmark against which all other bonds are compared. (Treasury *notes* work just like bonds except that notes are shorter maturities; Treasury *bills* were discussed in the section on cash.)

Treasury bonds are issued in minimum denominations of $1,000 and also in $5,000, $10,000, $100,000, and $1 million sizes. To invest in Treasury bonds, you put up your $1,000 (or more) and receive interest every six months.

Because literally trillions of dollars' worth of outstanding Treasury securities exist, the market for them is huge, and it is extremely easy to buy or sell them. But just because Treasuries are free from default risk does not mean you can't lose money on them. If you buy when rates are low and sell after rates have risen, as with all other bonds, the value of your Treasury bond will fall. On the other hand, if you buy when rates are high and sell after rates have fallen, you can capture a capital gain, on which you must pay a capital gains tax. All the interest you earn is exempt from state and local taxes, though you still must pay federal income tax on your Treasury bond interest.

In return for their safety, marketability, and tax advantages, you receive a lower yield than is available from other bonds. How much lower depends on current market conditions and the bonds to which you compare Treasuries. For conservative income-oriented investors, Treasuries are definitely worth considering.

Treasury Inflation Protection Securities (TIPS). TIPS are a relatively new investment vehicle and not as widely traded as other Treasury issues. TIPS offer the investor a hedge against inflation, because their principal value is adjusted to reflect changes in the consumer price index (CPI). Interest is calculated using the adjusted principal amount and paid semiannually.

TIPS are available directly from the Treasury. They are auctioned, as ten-year notes, quarterly by the U.S. Treasury. TreasuryDirect (http://www.treasurydirect.gov) has no fee transactions and allows the direct debiting of your bank account. Bonds are available in denominations of $1,000 and multiples thereof. Investors can invest up to $5 million at one auction. TIPS also can be bought through a bank or broker; however, you probably will be required to maintain an account and pay commission.

TIPS are exempt from state and local income taxes but subject to federal income taxes. Interest and any gains when the principal grows are considered reportable income and taxable in that year. TIPS work best in tax-advantaged accounts that allow tax deferral.

If the inflation-adjusted principal amount at maturity is less than the principal amount at issuance, the original principal amount is paid. Even in a deflationary period, the original principal is guaranteed. Prices of TIPS will rise and fall with the rise and fall of interest rates, just like ordinary bonds (although probably not as much).

Stop #2: U.S. Savings Bonds. Like Treasuries, savings bonds have the backing of the full faith and credit of the U.S. government, and the interest they pay is free from state and local taxes. Unlike Treasuries, though, savings bonds have the following features:

1. They are available in much smaller denominations. You can buy a savings bond at any bank or possibly through your company by payroll deduction for as little as $25 apiece.
2. Series EE savings bonds are issued at half their face value. For example, if you buy a $50 bond, you pay $25 for it. They have no set maturity date and pay no current interest, but you can redeem them any time.
3. You can swap non-interest-bearing Series EE bonds for a minimum of $500 worth of Series HH bonds, which pay cash interest.
4. The interest on education bonds is tax exempt (for people within certain gross income ranges), if you use it for college tuition for yourself, your spouse, or your children.

As you can see, savings bonds have a lot going for them. Appendix B offers more information on how they work.

Stop #3: Government Agency Securities. One notch riskier than Treasuries and U.S. Savings bonds are the securities issued by federal-government-backed agencies, such as Fannie Mae (the Federal National Mortgage Association), Ginnie Mae (the Government National Mortgage Association), and Freddie Mac (the Federal Home Loan Mortgage Corporation). Although they do not have the full faith and credit of the U.S. government behind them, a default is very unlikely.

They pay slightly higher yields than Treasury securities. They are not auctioned directly to the public, but are easy to buy through any traditional or discount brokerage firm. Depending on the agency, the bonds come in minimum denominations of $1,000 to $25,000.

Stop #4: Municipal Bonds. Although riskier than Treasury and possibly agency securities, *municipal bonds* (munis) are extremely popular. These bonds, issued by states, cities, counties, towns, villages, and taxing authorities of many types, have one feature that separates them from all other securities: the interest they pay is *totally free* from federal taxes. In addition, in almost every state, interest from bonds issued by that state is tax free to state residents; check to find out about the state in which you're interested in buying.

They offer *lower yields* than taxable government and corporate bond issuers must pay because investors (especially those in higher tax brackets) are satisfied to earn, for example, 4 percent tax free, compared to 6 percent on a Treasury, on which federal taxes are due. Munis are usually issued in minimum denominations of $5,000, though some are issued in lots as small as $1,000. Brokers usually require a minimum order of $5,000, but they prefer dealing in blocks of five bonds, or $25,000. Small orders invariably are hit with markups as high as 5 percent and therefore are generally not a good investment in small quantities.

Stop #5: Corporate Bonds. The next rung up the ladder of bond risk are bonds issued by corporations. Because corporations (no matter how solid they are financially) are perceived as vulnerable to changes in the business environment, the bonds they issue are considered riskier than government issues and therefore generally pay *a higher yield* than government issues of the same maturity. Still, only a tiny percentage of corporate bonds (typically less than 1 percent) ever default.

Depending on the financial creditworthiness of the issuing company, a corporate bond can yield 1 to 4 percentage points more than Treasuries of the same maturity. Again, most bond dealers don't like trading in lots of fewer than five bonds, or less than $5,000. For smaller lots, brokers' markups can be quite high.

Stop #6: Foreign Bonds. You need not restrict your search for solid, income-producing bonds to U.S. securities. The yields on foreign bonds can be significantly higher than those on similar domestic issues. It's important to note that the value of foreign bonds to U.S. investors can rise if the U.S. dollar falls against the foreign currencies and falls when the dollar rises. Finally, foreign government bonds are backed by the full faith and credit of their issuing countries. However, this guarantee has more weight coming from an industrialized country like Germany or France than a developing country like Kenya or Costa Rica.

Most U.S. brokers can sell foreign government bonds, though the easiest ones to trade are so-called *Yankee bonds,* which are issued in the United States by foreign governments and are denominated in dollars. Most foreign bonds, even Yankee bonds, come in minimum denominations much higher than the denominations of domestic issues (e.g., $25,000). Most individuals play this market by buying *mutual funds* that specialize in foreign bonds. Funds allow investors to avoid the complexities and high cost of buying individual foreign bonds, yet they offer high yields and the play on the U.S. dollar.

Stop #7: Zero-Coupon Bonds. These bonds (called *zeros* for short) get their name because the bond is issued with a 0 percent coupon rate. Instead of making regular interest payments, a zero is issued at a deep discount from its face value of 100, or $5,000. The return on a zero comes from the gradual increase in the bond's price from the discount to face value, which it reaches at maturity. This slow but steady rise in value yields three benefits:

1. You know exactly how much money you will receive when the bond matures.
2. You know exactly when you will receive that money.
3. You do not have to worry about reinvesting the small amounts of interest regular full-coupon bonds pay.

Very few investments can guarantee you will receive a specific dollar amount years from now. Because zeros have a specific schedule of appreciation, you can use a zero as an integral part of a financial plan to fund specific expenses years in advance. For example, if you are 40 and plan to retire at age 65, you can buy a 20-year zero that will mature on the day your company gives you the gold watch. On the other hand, zeros can be risky because they lock in a fixed reinvestment rate of interest for a long time, so their prices react to fluctuations in interest rates far more than any other type of bond.

If you want a diversified portfolio of zeros, you can buy shares in a *zero-coupon bond mutual fund* for a minimum of $1,000. One of the largest fund companies offering zero-coupon funds is American Century Investments (see Appendix B for contact information).

Stop #8: Convertible Bonds. Convertible bonds are hybrids; they have qualities of both bonds and stocks. Like *bonds,* they offer regular fixed income, although usually at a yield lower than straight bonds of the same issuer. Like *stocks,* convertibles offer significant appreciation potential and a way to benefit from the issuing companies' financial success. Convertible bonds are usually denominated in minimums of $1,000, although most brokers like to trade at least 10 bonds, or $10,000 worth, at a time. Convertibles offer no special tax breaks. All interest paid is fully taxable at the federal, state, and local levels. Although no taxes are due when you convert from a bond to common stock, you must pay all the normal taxes on the stock dividends. As with any other security, you must pay capital gains taxes if you sell a convertible for a profit. Finally, if you are considering the convertible only for the income, and you would not want to be caught holding the underlying stock, move on to another option.

Stop #9: Junk Bonds. The riskiest type of bond is known in the brokerage industry as *high-yield bonds,* but colloquially they are known as *junk bonds,* and are issued by corporations that have less than an investment-grade rating (i.e., Standard & Poor's and Fitch rate them below BBB, and Moody's rates them below Baa). This does not necessarily mean they are junk; only that for a variety of reasons investing in them is riskier than investing in other companies.

Although a low safety rating might be bad news for a company, it can be good news for investors because such bonds pay a substantially higher yield than securities issued by more financially stable corporations. How much more depends on which issuers you compare, but decent-quality junk bonds often yield between two and five percentage points more than investment-grade issues. That can translate into yields of 8 to 12 percent.

Stop #10: Bond Mutual Funds. If the process of choosing individual bonds seems too complicated, bond mutual funds might be right for you. (Mutual funds in general are discussed later in this chapter.)

The number one reason to buy a bond fund is for the simplicity of diversification. Mutual funds offer several advantages to bond investors:

► For the most part, the bond market is designed for large institutional players that buy blocks of bonds, millions of dollars at a time, rather than small investors who buy a few thousand dollars' worth of securities.

► Bonds can be difficult to trade in small lots, so bond mutual funds offer much better liquidity than do individual bonds.

► You can buy or sell a bond mutual fund at that day's net asset value (NAV) and not worry about taking a bad price on a solo bond.

► You also pay much less in commission costs than you would as an individual investor buying the same bonds—and you benefit from that professional's research on the bond market.

► If you wish, you can receive a monthly dividend check that will smooth out your cash flow. In contrast, individual bonds usually pay every six months.

► Finally, a bond fund is made up of tens, if not hundreds, of bonds, diversified by maturity, issuer, and quality. By spreading the risk, you soften considerably the impact of a negative development on any particular bond. You could not afford such a diversified portfolio on your own, and you are exposed to serious loss if a problem develops with an individual bond.

Compared to individual bonds, one disadvantage of bond funds is they (except for zero-coupon bond funds) never mature. Bonds within a portfolio might mature, but the fund is constantly reinvesting the proceeds, which means you have no guarantee that a bond fund will ever return your original purchase price.

Stop #11: Unit Investment Trusts (UITs). If you're looking for an income-oriented investment, you might consider UITs, sometimes called *defined asset trusts,* which buy a fixed portfolio of bonds and, unlike bond funds, hold them to maturity.

You can buy a UIT from any broker for a minimum of $1,000. You usually pay a sales charge of about 4–5 percent when you buy it, then minimal management expenses thereafter of .15 percent per year. Over the long term, though, these fees are less than the typical annual management fees of 1 percent or more on more actively managed bond funds. However, there are excellent bond funds available with no sales commissions and annual expenses of less than .05 percent. A few large brokerage firms, including Merrill Lynch, Nuveen, and Van Kampen Merritt, dominate the UIT business.

UITs offer several advantages:

▶ You buy into a widely diversified, professionally selected portfolio.

▶ You know exactly what assets the trust contains before you buy it.

▶ You receive fixed monthly income checks.

▶ You receive your principal back when the portfolio matures (usually in about 20 years) unlike a bond fund, which never matures.

▶ You can choose a UIT that fits your income needs. Many trusts specialize in municipal bonds and therefore pay tax-free interest; for investors who want extra security, some municipal trusts buy only insured bonds. In addition to municipal bonds, UITs buy mortgage-backed securities, high-quality corporate bonds, foreign bonds, and even junk bonds.

When shopping for a UIT, look carefully at the prospectus describing the portfolio. Notice the average maturity of the bonds, which may range from 10 to as many as 30 years. Inspect the bonds' safety ratings, making sure that they fall in the A category if you want to depend on the trust for income for many years. Determine what kind of call protection comes with the bonds in the portfolio. Ideally, you would like at least 10 years before the bonds can be redeemed. With a little homework, you may find a UIT that meets your needs for dependable monthly income (see Appendix B for resources).

▶ Route #3: Size Up Your Stock Investments

There are two basic ways to invest in the stock market: you can buy individual stocks, or you can invest in mutual funds. This section focuses on individual stocks; the next section covers the basics of mutual funds. This section also includes some of the basic terminology you should know.

Using the Price-Earnings (P/E) ratio to Evaluate Stock Prices

The most common way that investors value one stock against another within the same industry is by using the P/E ratio, which measures how much you, the investor, will pay for a dollar of earnings. To determine the P/E ratio, divide the stock's latest price by its earnings for the latest four quarters.

For example, if a stock is selling for $10 a share and it earned $1 a share last year, it has a P/E ratio of 10:

$10 Current stock price ÷ $1 Past earnings per share = 10 P/E

This P/E ratio, called the *trailing* P/E ratio because it is based on the past, is the figure shown in the newspaper listing under the heading "P/E."

A Six-Lane Highway: Different Types of Stocks for Different Goals

The following sections describe various types of stocks, generally categorized as cyclical, growth, income, out-of-favor, and value; we've also included IPOs (initial public offerings) as a sixth category. Once you know something about these and how they differ in terms of helping you achieve your specific financial goals, you should be able to determine which might be most appropriate for you, depending on your risk profile and financial objectives. Let's get started.

Stop and Go: Cyclical Stocks. Certain companies' fortunes are very closely tied to the ups and downs of the economy, and if you time purchases and sales of such company stocks well, you can profit handsomely. Cyclical stocks (so called because they ride the economic cycle) are typically found in such heavy industries as auto manufacturing, paper, chemicals, steel, and aluminum, which have high fixed costs in good times and bad.

The Fast Lane: Growth Stocks. The easiest way for most people to make money in stocks over the long term is to buy and hold shares in high-quality growth companies. If it is a true growth stock, its earnings will compound at 15 percent or more no matter what the overall economy is doing. Growth stocks can perform so admirably because their companies offer proprietary niche products or services and have well-known brand names, strong finances, and top-flight management.

So far, investing in growth stocks sounds like a breeze. But it isn't! The better the record a growth company establishes, the higher investors' expectations soar and the higher the stock's P/E ratio climbs. As long as the growth in earnings continues unabated, no problem occurs, but the moment the company reports a slight slip in its upward trajectory, the stock can take a pounding. As we stated earlier, one of the last investments you want to own is a growth stock about to disappoint investors' earnings expectations.

In general, the smaller the company, the greater its growth potential is, because it is easier to grow quickly from a small base than from a big one. But investing in stocks of smaller companies also entails more risk because they do not have the market positions as established larger companies do.

A Slow-but-Steady Lane: Income Stocks. Although most people think of stocks as a way to achieve *capital appreciation,* they can also provide *steady income* in the form of quarterly dividends. Companies that pay high dividends usually are well-established, profitable firms. Unlike faster-growing younger companies, which reinvest profits in their own businesses and pay little or no dividends, such firms traditionally pay out at least half their profits to shareholders in the form of dividends.

If you are thinking of buying an income stock, begin by analyzing the company's debt: if it's more than 50 percent of the company's equity, it may be a sign of trouble. You can also check the stock's rating with a reputable credit rating agency's ratings, such as *Standard & Poor's Stock Guide.* Any rating over B+ implies that the company is financially solid.

Don't be entranced by a stock that sports an above-average yield, say more than 8 percent. It may be high because the stock price has fallen in anticipation of a dividend cut or because the company is in the process of liquidation, and the high payouts are actually a return of shareholders' capital. Whatever the reason, be suspicious of stocks with ultra-high yields.

In the Ditch: Out-of-Favor Stocks. Since the way to make money in stocks is to buy low and sell high, then buying stocks when they are out of favor could be a good way to buy low. Investors are not always rational: Just as they can push the price of a growth stock to unrealistic heights, they can also pummel a stock that has momentarily slipped to unrealistically low prices. That's when bargain hunters swoop in. They attempt to sell out when the stock has recovered.

One way to spot out-of-favor stocks is by looking for low P/E ratios relative to their group. A P/E ratio of less than 10 may signal a lack of investors' interest in its prospects. They can be wrong, and the moment the company reports better-than-expected results, perceptions can change quickly, and the stock price can shoot up. Don't be tempted to buy any stock with a low P/E; some companies deserve their low valuation.

What you *should* look for is a stock with a fair chance at turnaround. You may infer that a recovery is on the way if sales and earnings are no longer deteriorating or if the company has a new product or service that has the potential to restart its growth. Another sign of life is if company executives are buying the stock themselves and whether they are increasing capital expenditures. If the people who know the company best are investing in it heavily, that could be a tip-off that recovery is at hand.

Hidden Shortcuts: Value Stocks. If you could buy a stock worth $10 for $8, would you do it? Most people would because they know they are buying something for less than it is currently worth. The key to value investing is being able to perceive when a stock's current price does not fully reflect the value of the enterprise and its assets. Those assets might include real estate, plant and equipment, inventories, reputation, brand names, patents, or even cash or stocks in other companies.

Value investors make money by buying when the stock's assets are *worth more than the stock's price* and selling when the value of the assets has been realized, which can happen when:

▶ A company is purchased by another company.
▶ The company is broken into pieces, leaving shareholders (e.g., you) with several stocks worth more separately than they were as a whole.
▶ The company's management finds a way to make the underused asset more profitable, thereby boosting the stock price.
▶ Investors finally realize the value of the company's assets, causing the stock price to rise.

You can get a sense of whether a stock is selling for less than its breakup value by looking at the company's book value per share, tangible assets like land or oil reserves, and financial assets including cash and securities. Another way to identify a value stock is to examine the firm's cash flow (profits plus depreciation) per share, and divide it by the current stock price. The lower the price-cash flow ratio, the more undervalued the stock. At a certain point, the cash the company is throwing off could make it a likely takeover target.

The Autobahn: Investing in Foreign Stocks. When buying stocks, you do not have to limit yourself to U.S. shares. In fact, the U.S. market currently accounts for only about a third of the world's total stock market value. Europe and Asia account for the other thirds. So if you restrict yourself to domestic stocks, you exclude two-thirds of the world's growth potential.

And you don't have to take an overseas trip to buy foreign stocks. In fact, hundreds of foreign-based-corporation stocks are available on the NYSE and AMEX, as well as on the Nasdaq NMS. When they trade here, foreign stocks are sold in the form of American depositary receipts (ADRs), which entitle the bearer to all dividends (converted into dollars) and capital gains that shareholders in the home country receive. ADRs must adhere to U.S. accounting rules, and, for all practical purposes, trade just like U.S. stocks.

Like any investment in foreign securities, ADRs can be affected by swings in the value of the U.S. dollar against other currencies. In general, a declining dollar boosts the price of an ADR while a rising dollar tends to depress the price of an ADR.

How to Buy and Sell Stock Shares

If you're going to buy individual stocks, you should know at least some of the necessary terminology. If you're not buying at the market price, here's a quick explanation of the five most common kinds of other orders you can give a broker to buy or sell shares.

Day order. This is an order to buy or sell a stock at a particular price on the day the order is placed. If the trade is not executed on that day, the order expires.

Good-till-canceled (GTC) order. A GTC order tells your broker to buy or sell a particular stock when it hits a specific price, whenever that might be. Such an order remains in effect until it is canceled. As long as the GTC order is in effect, it is known as an *open order.*

Limit order. With a limit order, you are telling your broker to buy or sell a particular stock at a certain price or better.

Stop order. With a stop order, you are trying to protect a profit or limit further losses. The most frequently used stop order, known as a *stop-loss order,* tells your broker to sell your stock if it hits a specific price, which is less than its current trading price. If a stock suddenly plummets, your order will be executed at the next market price after the stock hits the price you stated, which may be lower. If you want to make sure you get a specific price, you should place a limit order, but, in that situation, there is no guarantee that you'll be able to sell it at that price.

The risk in placing stop orders is that they may be executed because of a momentary setback in a stock's price. Therefore, do not set stop orders too close to the current market price. Most pros leave a 20 percent margin to avoid losing a stock that will bounce back.

▶ Follow Directions: A Roadmap to the Overall Stock Market

News reports about the stock market that you see or hear every day on television, on the radio, and in newspapers normally track the action of *stock indexes and averages,* not individual stocks. These reports can give you a sense of the general direction of stocks, though they will not tell you whether the stocks in your portfolio are up or down. Still, it is good to understand these indexes because they are commonly used as benchmarks for judging the performance of individual stocks. Each index is calculated slightly differently and measures a different sector of the market.

The Dow Jones Industrial Average. This is the most commonly quoted index: it tracks the movement of 30 of the largest blue chip stocks traded on the NYSE. When people say "How did the market do today?" they are usually referring to the performance of this average. The Dow Jones is a price-weighted average, so it is more affected by the movement of higher priced shares than by lower priced ones, no matter how many shares are outstanding. Dow Jones and Co., which maintains the average, also tracks utilities (electric and gas) in the Dow Jones Utilities Average and transportation stocks (airlines, railroads, and truckers) in the Dow Jones Transportation Average. The combined industrial, utilities, and transportation averages are called the Dow Jones Composite Average.

The Nasdaq Composite Index. This index tracks the movement of all companies traded on the Nasdaq market. These tend to be smaller, more volatile companies than the blue chips in the Dow Industrial Average or the S&P 500. The Nasdaq Composite is market-value weighted, which gives more influence to larger and higher priced stocks.

The Standard & Poor's 500 Index. The S&P 500 is the benchmark against which most portfolio managers compare themselves. It is composed of 500 blue chip stocks, separated by industry, so that almost all key industries are represented. The index always tracks 400 industrial company stocks, 60 transportation stocks, and 40 financial stocks, like banks or insurance companies.

Other Indexes. Other indexes include the NYSE Composite Index, the Wilshire 5,000 Equity Index, and foreign indexes.

An Alternate Route to Investing in Stocks:
Join (or Start) an Investment Club

If you don't want to choose stocks on your own, you have another alternative—starting an investment club or joining one that is already up and running. This is one way to make your investing less solitary: Get together with a group of people, pool your money, and decide on which stocks to buy or sell. The typical investment club has between five and 30 members, who usually start the club by contributing $100 each, then make a monthly deposit of $25 or $50.

Investing through such a club has several advantages:

1. You will hear about stocks you probably never would have heard about on your own. Because members of the club will come from all walks of life, they often will have insights into companies that are doing well in industries in which they work.
2. You can gain valuable experience from other members that you can apply to your own portfolio.
3. Through the club, you can be part of a more diversified portfolio than you could probably afford on your own.
4. The club will probably pay lower commissions than you would because it is buying more shares in each transaction.
5. You may make social or business contacts that are important beyond the investment club's scope: It's another new way to meet people.

Most successful investment clubs have a strategy that guides their stock selection. Some clubs concentrate on local stocks, whereas others look for growth stocks or undervalued companies. Whatever the style, it provides a framework for club members to research companies that might be of interest to its members. Appendix B offers information on how to get started in investing through an investing club.

▶ Route #4: Manage Your Mutual Funds for Maximum Value

If the process of selecting individual stocks seems a bit overwhelming, consider mutual funds, which is the most commonly used investment vehicle of most Americans and certainly most novice investors. They are easy to use and understand, and provide several great services at a low cost. Put simply, a stock mutual fund is a pool of money that a fund manager invests in stocks to achieve a specific objective.

Cruise-Control Investing: The Advantages of Mutual Funds

Mutual funds offer several key advantages over investing yourself in individual stocks. You certainly don't need to make your life any more complicated or difficult than it is at this time, so consider these advantages carefully when determining the right route for your investing plan.

A professional skilled in choosing stocks does all your work for you. Managers of stock mutual funds have instant access to information about every stock around the world at the push of a few computer keys. They work in companies where teams of research analysts pore over corporate quarterly and annual reports and managers and analysts visit company executives and factories to evaluate the firms' prospects firsthand.

A mutual fund gives you instant diversification. If you have only $1,000 or $5,000 to invest, that money will not buy many shares of a single stock, and it will certainly not buy many different stocks. By putting your money in only two or three stocks, you are exposed to the possibility that one of them will plummet in price, wiping out much of your investment capital. Instead, when you put your $1,000 or $5,000 in a mutual fund, your money buys into a portfolio that may include 50 or 500 stocks. Therefore, if one or two stocks in the portfolio get hit hard, your losses will be more limited because many of the other stocks will probably be going up at the same time.

There's a mutual fund for every financial goal and risk tolerance level. Once you've identified your goals and risk tolerance level, you can find a fund that fits your situation. The different types of funds are described in more detail later in this chapter, but in broad terms, there are funds designed for various degrees of growth and for varying levels of income, as well as funds that combine both growth and income objectives.

Transaction costs are much lower than buying individual stocks. When you invest in a mutual fund, you benefit from the brokerage commission rates paid by the fund company, which are far lower than you would pay to make the same trades. Over time, the lower transaction costs that the mutual fund pays will boost your return because you will have more money invested and less paid out in fees.

You can get into and out of a mutual fund easily. All it takes is a phone call to your broker, discount broker, or the fund. By law, a fund must allow you to buy shares at the fund's closing price on the day the fund gets your money. The closing price, called *net asset value* (NAV), is the value of the stock portfolio at the end of the day divided by the number of shares in the fund. Conversely, if you want to sell, the fund must redeem your shares at the NAV on the day you give your instructions. This instant liquidity can be a big advantage when you want to buy or sell stocks quickly.

Mutual funds can set up automatic systems to add or subtract money from your account or reinvest dividends and capital gains. Most mutual funds will automatically transfer a set amount—usually as little as $25—from your bank account or money-market mutual fund into the stock or bond fund of your choice on a regular basis, whether that be weekly, monthly, or annually.

In addition, as the fund captures capital gains by selling stocks at a profit, it disburses the proceeds as capital gains distributions. You can have the fund reinvest those distributions in more shares as well. Over time, the shares you own from reinvestment produce more shares, and the compounding effect can dramatically increase your capital. This is a simple way to invest on autopilot. You probably won't even miss the money from your checking account, but over time, you will build up your capital in the mutual fund.

On the other hand, if you are retired and want a regular income, most mutual funds will automatically withdraw a certain amount of money and send you a monthly check. This is called an *automatic withdrawal program,* which allows you to withdraw a regular amount of money from your funds every month. It is targeted mostly to retired people living off their funds.

You can easily switch from one fund to another within a fund family. Most mutual fund companies offer a broad array of mutual funds so that as your view of the stock market or your needs change, you can simply switch from one fund to another (not only between stock funds but also from stock funds to bond funds and money-market funds, which may act as havens when stock prices are falling). This is known as an *exchange.*

One disadvantage of a mutual fund is that, unless you hold shares in a tax-deferred retirement account, you must pay taxes on both reinvested dividends and capital gains in the tax year you receive them even though you have re-invested the money and have not sold your shares in the fund. Conversely, you may deduct any capital losses in the tax year you receive them.

Tolls or Toll-Free? Load vs. No-Load Mutual Funds

There are two basic types of mutual funds, differentiated by the method by which they are sold:

1. When you pay a commission to a salesperson, financial planner, or broker, that fee is called a *load.* Therefore this kind of fund is called a *load mutual fund* because you have to pay a commission to buy it.
2. The other kind of fund, called a *no-load fund,* is purchased directly through the mutual fund company or discount broker, with no salesperson involved. You can buy no-load shares through a discount broker (the best method), or online (the fastest method), or by calling the mutual fund company directly, usually at a toll-free number, and it sends you the necessary prospectus and application forms. Sending them back with a check opens your account.

Both no-load and load funds levy what is known as a *management fee* every year to compensate them for the services they render. The management fee, which ranges from as little as .2 percent of your assets to as much as 2 percent, is deducted from the value of the fund automatically.

Load Funds: Advantages and Disadvantages. The *advantage* of a load fund is that you receive advice from the salesperson on which fund to choose. Such advice may be worthwhile because it might be difficult for you to isolate the few funds that are best for your situation among the more than 17,000 funds in existence. Ideally, the salesperson helping you will not only tell you when to buy the fund but also when to sell your shares and move your money into a better fund.

The *disadvantage* of a load fund is that the commission you must pay immediately reduces the amount of money you have at work in the fund. The load can amount to as much as 8.5 percent of your initial investment, though many funds today charge 4 or 5 percent. Thus, for every dollar you sink into the fund, only 91.5 cents will earn money if you pay the full 8.5 percent load.

Hazard!
Other Mutual Fund Fees

In addition to front-end loads, there are other fees you should be aware of:

Back-end loads. To compete with no-load funds, many broker-sold funds now waive a charge when you buy them but hit you with a fee if you sell the funds before a particular period of time elapses. This is also called a back-end load or a *contingent deferred sales charge.*

Management fees. Both load and no-load funds have ongoing expenses, called annual fund operating expenses, that are paid by the investors. Management and investment advisory fees pay for managers and employees of the mutual fund company. A component of fund operating expenses, they average 1 percent annually.

Administrative costs. Also part of annual fund operating expenses, these fees are for recordkeeping, mailing, and customer service costs; they usually range from .2 percent to .4 percent.

Exchange fees. Some fund groups charge a fee if you exchange one fund for another within a fund family. The fee covers administrative costs and usually amounts to about $5 per transaction.

12b-1 fees. These charges, like management fees, are deducted automatically from the fund's assets each year. They cover distribution costs, which include advertising, promotion, literature, and sales incentives to brokers, and range from .25-1.25 percent of the fund's assets each year in general. Unless you invest in a fund that has a superb record or some other compelling reason to buy it, avoid funds that impose 12b-1 fees.

In the long run, expense ratios matter a great deal. In general, low-cost funds have beaten high-cost funds by substantial margins over long periods, regardless of which part of the market they targeted. When you see a huge difference in similar funds' returns, one fund is probably taking more risk or employing a different strategy. Does it make sense to pay an above-average expense ratio for that? Only if you think the fund's manager can keep generating returns that compensate you for the extra risk and the extra costs.

If you pay a 3 percent load, 96 cents of every dollar will be invested in stocks. In the short term, therefore, you are starting at a disadvantage over a no-load fund, where your whole dollar is at work from the beginning. Over a longer time period, however, if the load fund performs better than a no-load fund you might have picked, the up-front charge will pale in significance.

No-Load Funds: Advantages and Disadvantages. Clearly, the *advantage* of the no-load fund is that you have all of your money working for you from the moment you open your account.

The *disadvantage* of a no-load fund is that you will not receive much (if any) guidance on which fund to buy. When you call a no-load company's toll-free number, the phone representative can explain the differences among all of the firm's offerings. They can describe each fund's investment objective, track record, dividend yield, size in assets, management style, and fees, and the stocks currently in its portfolio. They are not licensed salespeople so they cannot advise you on which fund to buy. If you already have made up your mind based on information you have received about the fund from the fund company itself, reports in the press or on the Internet should not be a problem. There are also independent fee-only financial advisors who charge by the hour and provide specific investment advice regarding no-load funds as well as most other investment vehicles.

▶ The On Ramp: What You Should Know Before You Buy Shares in a Mutual Fund

Mutual fund companies have made it as easy as possible to open an account, but there is still a certain amount of legal paperwork you must go through in the process. To protect consumers and make sure they receive enough information about a fund, the SEC requires that potential fund shareholders receive a prospectus and an application form from the fund company.

Although you shouldn't expect the prospectus to compete with your favorite novel for light reading, it does contain several important facts you should understand before you give the fund any money:

▶ *The fund's investment objective.* It may be aiming for aggressive growth, steady income, or something in between.

▶ *The investment methods the fund uses to achieve its goals.* It may restrict itself to certain kinds of stocks, or it may use complex hedging strategies involving futures and options to prevent losses. The fund will also tell you what kinds of stocks it will not buy.

▶ *The fund's investment advisor.* The prospectus will outline the background of the fund company and usually tell you which portfolio manager or team of managers make the decisions about what stocks to buy and sell. Ultimately, the fund's performance is determined by the quality of the investment advisor.

▶ *The amount of risk the fund will assume.* Depending on the type of fund, the prospectus will reveal how volatile the fund's price is. The more risks the fund takes, the more its price will jump around.

▶ *The tax consequences of holding the fund.* For example, the prospectus will mention that you must pay taxes on all dividend and capital gains distributions.

▶ *A list of services provided by the fund.* The prospectus will tell you whether the fund is suitable for IRAs and Keogh accounts, whether you can re-invest dividends and capital gains automatically, and whether you can set up an automatic investment or withdrawal program. The prospectus will also tell you the minimum initial investment to get into the fund, as well as the minimum amount to make subsequent investments.

▶ *A financial summary of the fund's performance for the past 10 years, if it has been around that long.* A table will track the fund's price, dividends, and capital gains distributions that have been paid and expenses.

▶ *A listing of all fees.* This table will summarize the management fee, 12b-1 fees, sales charges, and any other fees charged to shareholders.

▶ Drive Carefully: Monitor Your Fund

Tracking the value of your fund holdings is simple. Just multiply the current price by the number of shares you own. For example:

500 Shares of Oppenheimer Total Return Fund × $10 per share
= $5,000 Total value

If you reinvest your distributions in more shares (which is probably a good idea), remember that the number of shares you own will continue to increase. Make sure to use the latest number of shares on your statement in calculating the value of your holdings.

The easiest way to determine the current price is to go online or call your fund company or broker. Most fund companies have automated voice systems so you can even call after working hours. You can also look up your fund's NAV at http://www.finance.yahoo.com or in a local or national newspaper.

The High Road or the Low Road? Choosing the Best Mutual Funds for You

Now that you understand the mechanics of buying and monitoring stock funds, it's time to determine which is best for you. As with all investments, before you sink your money into any fund, you should review your financial goals and your risk tolerance level at this point in your life. The following paragraphs describe different categories of stock funds.

High-Risk Funds

Here's a quick overview:

1. *Aggressive growth funds.* These funds buy stocks of fast-growing companies or other companies that have great capital gains potential, sometimes even in bankrupt or depressed companies, anticipating a rebound. Such funds often trade stocks frequently, hoping to catch small price gains.
2. *Foreign stock funds.* These funds buy stocks of corporations based outside the United States. In addition to the usual forces affecting stock prices, fluctuations in the value of the U.S. dollar against foreign currencies can dramatically affect the price of these funds' shares, particularly over the short term.
3. *Sector funds.* Sector funds buy stocks in just one industry (or sector) of the economy; for example, technology stocks, utilities, and natural resources. Because these funds are not diversified outside of their sector, they soar or plummet on the fate of the industry in which they invest.
4. *Small-company growth funds.* Such growth funds invest in stocks of small companies, typically with a total market value of $1 billion or less. These companies may have enormous growth potential, but their stocks are much less established—and therefore riskier—than large companies in mature industries.

Moderate-Risk Funds

1. *Growth funds.* Growth funds invest in shares of well-known growth companies that usually have a long history of increasing earnings. Because

the stock market fluctuates, growth funds rise and fall as well, just not as much as funds holding smaller, less proven stocks.

2. *Equity-income funds.* Such funds own shares in stocks that pay higher dividends than do growth funds. Whereas a growth fund's payout may be 0 to 1 percent, an equity-income fund might yield 2 or 3 percent. That higher yield tends to cushion the fund's price when stock prices fall. When stock prices rise, equity-income funds tend to increase less sharply than do pure growth funds. A slightly more aggressive version of an equity-income fund is called a *growth and income fund* or a *total return fund* because it strives for gains from both income and capital appreciation.

3. *Index funds.* These funds buy the stocks that make up a particular index to allow investors' returns to match the index; the most popular of these is the S&P 500. The management fees of an index fund are much lower than those of other stock funds. Proponents of index funds argue that because many money managers fail to match or beat the S&P 500 each year, investors can come out ahead by just matching the index.

4. *Socially conscious funds.* Such funds look for companies that meet certain criteria, such as advancing minority and female employees or helping clean up the environment. These funds screen out stocks of companies that are major polluters, defense contractors, or promoters of gambling or tobacco.

Low-Risk Funds

1. *Balanced funds.* Balanced funds keep a fairly steady mix of high-dividend, large company stocks and quality bonds. This allows the funds to pay a fairly high rate of current income and still participate in the long-term growth of stocks.

2. *Asset allocation funds.* These funds have the latitude to invest in stock, bonds, or cash instruments, depending on the fund manager's market outlook. If they think stock prices are about to fall, the manager can shift all the fund's assets into cash instruments. If they think stock prices are about to rise, the manager can move all the fund's assets into stocks. Usually, the fund will always have some money in stocks, bonds, and cash, which tends to stabilize its performance.

3. *Utilities funds.* Such funds buy shares in electric, gas, telephone, and water utilities. Because all these companies are regulated monopolies, they

have steady earnings and pay high dividends. Utilities funds are subject to swings in interest rates, however. Nonetheless, for a high-yielding and relatively stable stock fund, a utilities fund is worth considering.

▶ An Alternate Route: Investing in Closed-End Mutual Funds

So far, we've discussed open-end funds. Another variety of fund is called a *closed-end fund*. Like open-end funds, closed-end funds offer the advantages of professional management, diversification, convenience, and automatic reinvestment of dividends and capital gains.

The difference between the two types of funds comes in the way you buy shares. Open-end funds create new shares as more money is invested in them. When cash is taken out of the fund, the number of outstanding shares shrinks. The portfolio manager therefore is faced with an ever-changing pool of assets that can be small one month and huge the next, with millions of dollars flowing in and out. This pattern of volatile cash flow can severely harm the fund's performance because, if the fund manager stays fully invested, the manager must buy stocks when prices are high and sell them when prices are low.

Closed-end funds are designed to avoid this problem. Instead of continually creating and redeeming shares, these funds issue a limited number of shares, which trade on the New York or American Stock Exchange or on the Nasdaq National Market System. Instead of dealing with the fund company directly when you buy or sell shares, as you do with open-end funds, you trade closed-end shares with other investors, just as you do any publicly traded stock. You pay traditional or discount brokerage commissions to buy and sell them, and the fund's price is listed in the newspaper's stock tables or on the Internet every day.

You should assess two factors when you buy a closed-end fund:

1. The fund manager's record in choosing winning stocks that allow the fund to achieve its investment objective.
2. Whether you are buying the fund at a premium or a discount. Some investors' entire strategy with closed-end funds is to buy them at a discount and wait for them to rise to a premium, at which point they sell.

▶ Route #5: Realistically Assess Your Real Estate

Widows and widowers tend to stay in the homes they shared with their spouses, for both emotional and financial reasons. If you own a home, it is costly and disruptive to sell it and move to a smaller place when your spouse dies. If you want to sell, though, we'll cover that later in this section.

First Stop: Going in "Reverse" so that You Can Stay in Your Home

One way to remain in your home but receive income from the property is to assume a reverse mortgage, if you own your home free and clear. Instead of borrowing against your equity and paying interest, you contract with a bank to convert some of your home equity to cash while you retain ownership. These are called reverse mortgages because unlike traditional mortgages, the *bank* makes payments to *you*.

You can take your proceeds in a lump sum, in monthly checks, or through a line of credit you can tap whenever you want. The amount you can borrow depends on your age, the value of the equity in your home, and the interest rate charged by the lender. Some charge a fixed rate of interest, whereas others charge a variable rate. Unless you take a lump sum, the amount of interest you owe increases every month. Over time, the interest owed can become considerable, and your equity stake can shrink dramatically. However, a reverse mortgage can be a good way to use the equity in your home.

To obtain a reverse mortgage, you normally must pay closing costs and insurance premiums and sometimes a monthly service fee. The reverse mortgage comes due when you die, sell the home, or move permanently when you or your heirs must pay off the loan, or the bank will take title to your home.

All payments you receive from a reverse mortgage (technically, they are loan advances) are considered nontaxable income. Therefore, they do not lower your Social Security or Medicaid benefits. On the other hand, the interest you pay on reverse mortgages is not tax deductible until you pay off all or part of your reverse mortgage debt.

A related technique to tap your home's equity is to assume a *reverse annuity mortgage* (RAM) where you use the proceeds generated by a mortgage on your home to buy an annuity from an insurance company. The insurer pays the interest on your mortgage and sends the rest of the money to you in monthly installments. Upon your death, the insurer usually sells your home and repays the mortgage balance. Remaining funds are passed on to your heirs through your estate.

The amount of monthly income you receive from a RAM depends on the interest rate the insurer pays, your life expectancy, and the equity you have accumulated in your home. In general, the monthly payment you receive is usually less than a traditional reverse mortgage. For more detailed information on how reverse mortgages work and which institutions currently grant them, see Appendix B.

Stop #2: If You Decide to Sell Your Home

When the time comes to sell your home, you must do just as much homework as you did when you bought the property. The first step in getting the highest price possible for your home is to obtain a realistic appraisal of its current value. If you have paid little attention to the market for the past several years, you may have an outdated sense of what your home is worth.

You can get a feel for the market by scanning newspaper ads or the Internet for similar properties and by visiting nearby open houses. Real estate agents will be glad to give you a free assessment of your home's strengths, weaknesses, and fair price range. For a fee, you can also obtain a professional appraiser's opinion.

If you want to avoid the real estate broker's fee, you can try to sell your home yourself with newspaper ads and a For Sale sign on your front lawn. Although you will have to deal with browsers and people unqualified to buy your property, you may be lucky enough to find someone who falls in love with your home and places a bid on it.

If you're located in an active real estate market, you might be able to sell within a few weeks. It is always best, however, to sell your home before you buy another property. You don't want to owe two mortgage payments if your home sells more slowly than you anticipate.

More and more states require that you disclose all of your home's problems in writing to prospective buyers. The document covers a property's structure, utilities (such as plumbing, air-conditioning, and water system), and municipal status (such as building permits, zoning restrictions, certificate of occupancy, and property tax rates). If the buyer signs this sales disclosure form acknowledging that they have been informed of the home's

Tollbooth 5.1

Net Proceeds Worksheet

Gross Equity	$ Amount	Total
Sale Price of Property	$ _____	
Minus Remaining Mortgage Balance	(_____)	
Minus Other Home-Related Debts	(_____)	
Total Gross Equity		$ _____
Selling and Closing Costs		
Escrow or Other Fees	$ _____	
Legal and Document Preparation Fees	_____	
Title Search and Insurance Fees	_____	
Transfer Taxes	_____	
FHA, VA, or Lender Discounts	_____	
Mortgage Prepayment Penalties	_____	
Real Estate Taxes Owed	_____	
Appraisal Fees	_____	
Survey Fees	_____	
Termite and Other Pest Inspection Fees	_____	
Fees for Repair Work Required by Sales Contract	_____	
Home Protection or Warranty Plan Fees	_____	
Unpaid Assessments	_____	
Real Estate Commissions	_____	
Other Selling or Closing Costs	_____	
Total Selling And Closing Costs		$ _____
Total Gross Equity		
(minus)		$ _____
Total Selling And Closing Costs		(_____)
(equals)		
Net Proceeds		$ _____

problems, the buyer has little right to sue you later if any problems crop up for any of the items listed.

If you cannot or do not want to sell your home on your own, bring in several real estate agents to compete for your listing. Unless you deal with a flat-fee or discount broker, you must pay the agent a commission of 6 to 7 percent of your home's selling price.

When you sell your home, either on your own or through an agent, deduct all selling and closing costs from the gross sales price to arrive at your net proceeds. The worksheet in Tollbooth 5.1 lists some of the costs you might incur and helps you determine your profit.

▶ Looking Ahead

When updating or creating a new long-term financial plan for investing, first determine what level of risk you're comfortable with, then decide where you want to invest your money:

- ▶ in cash, which provides low interest but maximum liquidity (meaning you can access it at any time, without penalty): You can choose among a traditional savings account, interest-bearing checking, money market deposit accounts and money-market mutual funds, Treasury bills, and CDs.
- ▶ in bonds, of various types (this chapter described a dozen): Here you need to invest at least $1,000 in most types (except for savings bonds, which run as low as $25 each, though some bonds require as much as $25,000 minimum investment), for relatively low risk.
- ▶ in stocks, either buy individual stocks (in which case, you should choose between six different types: cyclical, growth, income, out-of-favor, value, and IPOs, and you'll need to know how to value a company's stock and how to buy and sell), or in mutual funds, in which case you should know something about what stocks comprise the fund and what fees you'll have to pay.
- ▶ in real estate, which is primarily the home you're living in. We've provided some information on reverse mortgages, if you want to stay in your home, as well as some guidance if you want to sell your home and move on down the road.

Appendix A

An Itinerary

Here's a quick review of what to do, as you set out on the road to getting your finances in order during this difficult time.

► Stop 1: Organize Your Finances

► Locate important financial papers and set up a recordkeeping system: Consolidate all your important information in one worksheet, including telephone numbers and addresses of all family members and professional advisors (bankers, financial planners/advisors, insurance agents, etc.) whom you should contact immediately, as well as information on all relevant financial records, such as bank accounts, retirement plans, mutual funds, stock certificates, bonds, real estate, wills, tax records, etc.

► Get organized and pay your bills. Consider online banking, to make this process easier during the first few months of your loss.

► Find an accountant (if you don't already have one) to help you with your new tax status and filing any tax returns.

► Contact all relevant financial institutions, including your bank, your spouse's employer, mortgage holders, credit card companies, etc.

► Stop 2: Develop a Budget for the Next Phase of Your Life

► Tally your assets, including all cash and investments (stocks, bonds, etc.), retirement funds, real estate, valuables, and other personal property.

► Tally up all your liabilities—i.e., your bills, mortgage payments, debts, unpaid taxes, outstanding loans, etc.

► Calculate your net worth by subtracting your liabilities from your assets. Now you know where you stand, financially, so you can make short- and long-term financial decisions and plans.

▶ Analyze your cash flow: How much money is coming in (from your spouse's estate and your own salary, etc.) and your current expenses, including everything from fixed expenses (such as your mortgage) to flexible expenses (such as expensive gifts to others)—again, to get a sense of where your money comes and goes.

▶ Create a yearly budget, to map out the big picture of your irregular, occasional, non-monthly, and periodic expenses at a glance (e.g., home and car expenses, medical and dental checkups, gifts at holidays, etc.).

▶ Create a monthly budget, as a smaller map of your fixed monthly expenses (e.g., your mortgage, car loan payment, gas/electric bill, phone bills, cable TV, etc.).

▶ Stop 3: Develop a Long-Term Financial Plan and Update Your Estate Plan

▶ Update your will and estate plans, to ensure that your children or other heirs and beneficiaries are provided for.

▶ Designate an executor for your will and a legal guardian for your minor children, and make sure both people agree to serve in those capacities.

▶ If you don't already have one, hire an estate lawyer to help you with this process: Don't go it alone at this difficult time of your life. You want to ensure that your wishes are carried out appropriately, so bring in an expert.

▶ Again, if you don't already have one, find a financial advisor to help you plan for your retirement, your children's education, or other long-term financial goals you have. Choose this person carefully (especially now, when you're most vulnerable). Make sure they have the right background and experience and find out how they need to be compensated, and make sure you're comfortable entrusting your financial plans to the advisor you ultimately choose.

▶ Stop 4: Make Sure You Have Enough Insurance for All Your Assets

▶ Update your life insurance: Calculate the benefits you'll be receiving from your spouse's insurance policies; then make sure your survivors will get what they need from your own life insurance, in terms of monetary amount and type of policy.

▶ Update your health insurance policies—whether you have a traditional fee-for-service reimbursement plan, an HMO, a PPO, Medicare, Medigap, or other specialized policies.

▶ Update your disability and long-term care insurance: Calculate how much money you would need, should something happen to you and you can't work.

▶ If you haven't done it recently (or if you've made any changes), update your homeowners insurance: It may be the last thing on your mind right now, but you need to make sure nothing happens to your home during this difficult time. Make sure you're covered for all contingencies.

▶ Finally, make sure you have up-to-date car insurance, to protect you against both damage to your car as well as personal injury for you and anyone driving your car.

▶ Stop 5: Reassess Your Investment Plans and Goals

▶ Decide how you want to allocate your savings and investments: in cash, bonds, individual stocks, mutual funds, and/or real estate.

▶ Consider how much money you want to invest in cash vehicles—i.e., savings accounts, interest-paying checking accounts, money market accounts, money-market mutual funds, Treasury bills, and CDs.

▶ Determine whether you want to invest in bonds, and, if so, what type: Treasuries, U.S. savings bonds, munis, corporate bonds, mortgage-backed securities, zeros, bond funds, or others.

▶ Know how to buy and sell shares in individual stocks, if that's the course you want to take, and understand which types best meets your goals (cyclical stocks, growth stocks, income-producing stocks, value stocks, out-of-favor stocks, foreign stocks, or IPOs. Keep in mind you should have a balanced portfolio, rather than simply investing in just one type of stock, or for that matter, bonds, etc.).

▶ Recognize the advantages of investing in stock mutual funds, and learn the basics of the fees involved and how to get started.

▶ Don't forget the value of your home as a real estate investment: Decide whether you want to stay put or move on, and know the benefits and drawbacks of each scenario.

Appendix B

The Best of *Surviving the Loss of a Spouse*: A Resource Guide

▶ Bibliography

The following books were used as resources for this book. In addition, there are lists of other books and Web sites that offer more detailed information on some of the topics covered in this book. We hope you find all these resources useful.

Briles, Judith, Edwin C. Schilling III, and Carol Ann Wilson. *The Dollars and Sense of Divorce*. Chicago: Dearborn Trade Publishing, 1998.

Garrett, Sheryl. *Just Give Me the Answers*. Chicago: Dearborn Trade Publishing, 2004.

Goodman, Jordan E. *Everyone's Money Book*, 3rd ed. Chicago: Dearborn Trade Publishing, 2001.

Lawrence, Judy. *The Budget Kit: The Common Cents Money Management Workbook*, 4th ed. Chicago: Dearborn Trade Publishing, 2004.

Ventura, John. *The Will Kit*, 2nd ed. Chicago: Dearborn Trade Publishing, 2002.

▶ Recommended Additional Books

Charles Schwab's New Guide to Financial Independence: Practical Solutions for Busy People by Charles R. Schwab (New York: Three Rivers Press, Random House, 2004). A basic book for people who recognize the importance of investing but know little or nothing about how to do it. Explains the ins and outs of planning an investment, choosing the instruments, and looking out for taxes.

Ernst & Young's Personal Financial Planning Guide by Martin Nissenbaum, Barbara J. Raasch, and Charles L. Ratner (Hoboken, NJ: John Wiley &

Sons, Inc., 2004). Covers fundamentals of financial planning and in the second half focuses on major life events (marriage, homebuying, starting a business, raising a family, retirement), showing how each event or stage in life affects one's current financial picture.

Personal Finance for Dummies by Eric Tyson (Indianapolis, IN: John Wiley & Sons, Inc., 2003). Includes financial planning advice for dealing with life changes and finances, budgets, savings accounts, tax implications, insurance, and more.

Smart Money: How to Be Your Own Financial Manager by Ken and Doria Dolan (New York: Random House, 1988). A breezy guide to personal finance, presented mostly in question-and-answer format.

Banking Online for Dummies by Paul A. Murphy (Indianapolis, IN: John Wiley & Sons, Inc., 1999). Covers all online banking options from checking account balances to paying bills to importing data into your financial software package. Helps you locate your bank on the Web, transfer funds, pay bills, review your accounts, and manage your money with the popular financial software packages.

The Smart Woman's Guide to Spending, Saving, and Managing Money by Ellie Williams Clinton and Diane Pearl (New York: Harper Torch, 1988). Describes how to make a budget, put money away, get the best mortgage, invest, consolidate debts, and cut credit card addiction.

Martindale-Hubbell Law Directory (New Providence, NJ: Martindale-Hubbell, 2003). A complete listing of U.S. and international lawyers by state and specialty.

The Online Broker and Trading Directory by Larry Chambers and Karen Johnson (New York: McGraw-Hill, 1999). Provides readers with a profile of the 100 top brokerages in the nation. Readers will find the best sites for technical analysis and brokerages with the best commissions and fastest trade executions. Explains online trading and Wall Street terms and examines the services offered by online trading companies.

The Right Way to Hire Financial Help: A Complete Guide to Choosing and Managing Brokers, Financial Planners, Insurance Agents, Lawyers, Tax Preparers, Bankers, and Real Estate Agents, 2nd ed. by Charles A. Jaffe (Cambridge, MA: The MIT Press, 2001). The basics of hiring and managing brokers, financial planners, insurance agents, lawyers, tax preparers, bankers, and real estate agents, plus questions to ask.

Smart Questions to Ask Your Financial Advisers by Lynn Brenner and Mark Matcho (Princeton, NJ: Bloomberg Press, 1997). In addition to listing questions for financial advisors, it includes questions to ask when purchasing a house, selling a house, and purchasing insurance.

Using a Lawyer... And What to Do If Things Go Wrong: A Step-by-Step Guide by Kay Ostberg (New York: Random House, 1990). A complete guide to shopping for and working with a lawyer. Provides sample fee agreements and a state-by-state list of lawyer grievance committees.

For more information on creating/updating your will

The Complete Guide to Wills, Estates & Trusts by Alexander A. Bove (New York: Owl Books/Henry Holt and Co., 2000). Details the most up-to-date laws and benefits for a variety of trusts, including educational trusts, Medicaid trusts, asset protection trusts, and more.

The Complete Idiot's Guide to Wills and Estates by Stephen M. Maple (New York: Penguin Putnam, 2002). Lays out a whole process, including step-by-step directions for writing a will, language to be used in letters to executors and heirs, and power of attorney.

The Complete Probate Guide by Martin M. Shenkman (Hoboken, NJ: John Wiley & Sons Inc., 1999). Provides advice, sample forms, checklists, tips, and definitions for the newly widowed or heir; explains all aspects of probate, including state-by-state coverage.

The Complete Will Kit, 3rd ed. by F. Bruce Gentry and Jens C. Appel III (Hoboken, NJ: John Wiley & Sons Inc., 2001). Contains all the forms you need to write a will, as well as state-by-state legal requirements for wills.

8 Ways to Avoid Probate: The Plain English Guide to Saving Your Family Thousands of Dollars by Mary Randolph (Berkeley CA: Nolo Press, 2004). Explanation of probate avoidance techniques

Estate Planning: Step by Step (Barron's Legal-Ease Series) by Martin M. Shenkman (Hauppage, NY: Barron's Educational Series, 1997). A guide to all the legal and tax aspects and financial details of estate planning.

Estate Planning Made Easy, 2nd ed. by David T. Phillips and Bill S. Wolfkiel (Chicago, IL: Dearborn Trade, 1997). Offers the basics of estate planning and shows the advantages of early estate planning.

Everything Your Heirs Need to Know: Organizing Your Assets, Family History, Final Wishes, 3rd ed. by David S. Magee and John Ventura (Chicago, IL: Dearborn Trade, 1998). A step-by-step workbook for anyone planning an orderly transition and transfer of assets; also enables readers to assemble information about personal history, final wishes, insurance policies, bank accounts, real estate, wills, and trust agreements.

How to Make Your Own Will, 2nd ed. by Mark Warda (Naperville, IL: Sphinx Publishing, 2000). This is a self-help law kit with forms.

Maximize Your Inheritance: For Widows, Widowers & Heirs by Jarratt G. Bennett (Chicago, IL: Dearborn Trade, 1999). Provides surviving spouses and heirs with solutions to getting financially organized, immediate concerns, claiming everything that's yours from private as well as government sources, and settling the estate.

9 Ways to Avoid Estate Taxes by Mary Randolph and Denis Clifford (Berkeley, CA: Nolo Press, 1999). Presents nine major methods people can use to avoid or reduce federal estate taxes.

Nolo's Simple Will Book, 5th ed. by Denis Clifford (Berkeley, CA: Nolo Press, 2003). Explains why you need a will and shows what the will must cover to be legally valid. Discusses guardianship, creating trusts, and avoiding probate. Includes a CD with forms.

Plan Your Estate: Absolutely Everything You Need to Know to Protect Your Loved Ones, 5th ed. by Denis Clifford and Cora Jordan (Berkeley, CA: Nolo Press, 2000). Deals with many issues related to planning an estate: children and probate; estate and gift taxes; second marriages and a variety of trust options; married people versus single; joint tenancy; life insurance; retirement benefits; taxes; and wills.

Probate and Settling an Estate by James John Jurinski (Hauppage, NJ: Barron's Educational Series, 1997). A general review of the probate, the executor's role, understanding a will's provisions, managing property, paying creditors and taxes, closing an estate, and dealing with special problems.

Employee Benefits, 6th ed. by Burton T. Beam, Jr. and John McFadden (Chicago, IL: Dearborn Trade, 2000). Comprehensive explanation of employee benefits, updated to incorporate the Health Insurance Portability and Accountability Act and the implications of the latest tax laws.

Fundamentals of Employee Benefits Programs, 5th ed. (Washington, DC: Employee Benefit Research Institute, 1997). A comprehensive overview of all major employee benefits programs, including Social Security, pension plans, salary reduction plans, profit-sharing plans, employee stock ownership plans, SEPs, IRAs, health insurance, dental insurance, drug prescription plans, group life insurance, disability insurance, education assistance, FSAs, MSAs, and temporary leave programs.

Solutions Handbook: For Personal Financial Planning, Business Planning, Employee Benefits, Estate Planning by Genevieve Ferraro, Sheryl Lilke, and R. Newkirk (Chicago, IL: Dearborn Financial Publishing, 1995).

For more information on insurance

Buying Insurance by Stuart Schwartz and Craig Conley (Capstone Press, Mankato, MN, 1998).

How to Get Your Money's Worth in Home and Auto Insurance by Lynn Brenner and Barbara J. Taylor (New York: McGraw-Hill, 1990). Shows readers how to quickly and easily figure out their personal insurance needs on their houses and cars.

How to Insure Your Home: A Step by Step Guide to Buying the Coverage You Need at Prices You Can Afford by the Silver Lake editors (Los Angeles: Merritt Publishing, 1996). Explains the mechanics and pricing structures of standard insurance. Offers guidelines for comparing various policies and provides tips and tactics for getting the best coverage for the money.

How to Insure Your Life: A Step by Step Guide to Buying the Coverage You Need at Prices You Can Afford by Reg Wilson and the Silver Lake editors (Los Angeles: Merritt Publishing, 1996). Provides tips and tactics to help people get the best life insurance coverage for their money. Includes easy-to-use forms.

The Complete Idiot's Guide to Buying Insurance and Annuities by Brian H. Breuel (New York: Penguin Putnam, 1996). Provides simple explanations and illustrations to help the reader understand insurance jargon and includes tips to advise the reader on insurance and annuity matters.

The Insider's Guide to HMOs: How to Navigate the Managed-Care System and Get the Health Care You Deserve by Alan J. Steinberg (New York: Plume Books, 1997). Explains the differences between various health care plans, evaluates the doctors in different systems, and shows how one can pay the best rate for the better HMO. Also explains all of the terms, conditions, and restrictions common to HMOs and uses case histories to clarify and illustrate the suggestions and tips given.

Winning the Insurance Game: The Complete Consumer's Guide to Saving Money by Ralph Nader and Wesley J. Smith (New York: Main Street Books/Doubleday/Random House, 1993). Discusses how to get the best coverage and fair prices for auto, health, homeowners, and life insurance. Also explains government insurance programs, including Social Security and Medicare, as well as specialized insurance coverage such as senior citizens' insurance, workers' compensation, and prepaid legal insurance.

For more information on investing

All About Stocks: The Easy Way to Get Started by Esme E. Faerber (New York: McGraw-Hill, 1999). Covers stock market basics for newcomers with concise and understandable answers to today's most-asked stock market questions.

Beating the Street by Peter Lynch (New York: Simon & Schuster, 1994). Written by the legendary manager of the Fidelity Magellan Fund, who explains how he picks stocks. Details how he first heard about companies and where he found the information so critical to deciding whether to invest in them. Also offers advice on buying mutual funds and putting together an investment program.

Buying Stocks Without a Broker by Charles B. Carlson (New York: McGraw-Hill, 1996). Shows how individual investors can avoid paying broker's commissions by buying stock directly from the issuing company.

The Complete Idiot's Guide to Online Investing by Douglas Gerlach (New York: Penguin Putnam, 1999). Provides users with an easy-to-understand book on the basics of investing and computing, researching options, and using the Internet for portfolio management.

The Dictionary of Finance and Investment Terms by John Downes and Jordan E. Goodman (Hauppage, NY: Barron's Educational Series, 2002). The standard reference work of finance and investment, defining more than 5,000 terms in simple language.

The First Time Investor: How to Start Safe, Invest Smart & Sleep Well, 3rd ed. by Larry Chambers and Dale Rogers (New York: McGraw-Hill, 2004). Packed with easy-to-use information on every aspect of investing.

If You're Clueless About the Stock Market and Want to Know More by Seth Godin (Chicago, IL: Dearborn Trade, 2001).

Investing Online for Dummies, 4th ed. by Kathleen Sindell (Indianapolis, IN: John Wiley & Sons, Inc., 2002). Covers all the basics for the online investor, including setting up stock screens, selecting mutual funds, looking for IPOs, and online banking and trading.

How to Invest the Smart Way: In Stocks, Bonds, and Mutual Funds by Stephen L. Littauer (Chicago, IL: Dearborn Trade, 1998). How to achieve financial independence with as little as $50 a month to invest. Starts from basics and covers planning, strategies, techniques, and markets. Covers stocks, bonds, and mutual funds.

Investment Clubs: A Team Approach to the Stock Market by Kathryn Shaw (Chicago, IL: Dearborn Financial Publishing, 1995). A simple step-by-step guide that shows the investor how to start and run a successful money-making investment club.

Business Week Guide to Mutual Funds, 5th ed. by Jeffrey M. Laderman (New York: McGraw-Hill, 1995). Explains the different types of funds, recommends investment strategies for all ages, and explains why some funds may work better than others.

Buying Mutual Funds for Free by Kirk Kazanjian (Chicago, IL: Dearborn Trade, 1997). How to put together a diversified portfolio of the world's finest funds by opening an account at one of the discount brokers and selecting from the list of no-load, no transaction-fee offerings.

How to Buy Mutual Funds the Smart Way by Stephen Littauer (Chicago, IL: Dearborn Trade, 1992). A thorough introduction to mutual funds for the financial do-it-yourselfer who likes to be in control, reduce costs, and rely on their own judgment.

Mutual Funds for Dummies, 3rd ed. by Eric Tyson and James C. Collins (Indianapolis, IN: John Wiley & Sons, Inc., 2001). Market data and analysis about the ever-changing world of mutual funds. Simplifies financial planning and points to the mutual fund investments best suited for you.

All about Bonds and Bond Mutual Funds: The Easy Way to Get Started, 2nd ed. by Esme Faerber (New York: McGraw-Hill, 1999). Simple, comprehensive book about bonds and bond funds. Includes new material on bond mutual funds, tax-free municipal bonds, international bonds, and bond funds.

Beating the Dow with Bonds: A High-Return, Low-Risk Strategy for Outperforming the Pros Even When Stocks Go South by Michael B. O'Higgins and John McCarty (New York: HarperBusiness, 2000).

Getting Started in Bonds, 2nd ed. by Sharon Saltzgiver Wright (Hoboken, NJ: John Wiley & Sons, 2003). Guide for the novice bond investor. Covers basic concepts as well as explains the broader factors that affect bond prices; well organized with solid fundamental bond information.

For more information on real estate

All about Mortgages: Insider Tips for Financing and Refinancing Your Home, 3rd ed. by Julie Garton-Good (Chicago, IL: Dearborn Trade, 2004). Provides an easy-to-follow road map through the twists and turns of the home mortgage loan process.

All about Real Estate Investing: The Easy Way to Get Started, 2nd ed. by William Benke and Joseph M. Fowler (New York: McGraw-Hill, 2001). Practical guide to profitable real estate investing. Covers houses, apartments, and commercial real estate.

Buy It, Fix It, Sell It: PROFIT! 2nd ed. by Kevin C. Meyers (Chicago, IL: Dearborn Trade, 2003)

Dress Your House for Success: 5 Fast, Easy Steps to Selling Your House, Apartment, Condo for the Highest Possible Price! by Martha Webb and Sarah Parsons Zackheim (New York: Three Rivers Press/Random House, 1997). Lots of ideas, checklists, and drawings to help the reader move property.

The For Sale by Owner Kit, 5th ed. by Robert Irwin (Chicago, IL: Dearborn Trade, 2005). Explains how to set a realistic price; prepare a home for sale; promote the home with effective signs and advertising; find buyers; deal with documents, agents, and brokers; and close the deal.

The Homeseller's Kit, 5th ed. by Edith Lank with Dena Amoruso (Chicago, IL: Dearborn Trade, 2001). Tells how to list your house with or without an agent and how to price your property.

The Homeseller's Survival Guide, by Kenneth W. Edwards (Chicago, IL: Dearborn Trade, 1995). Identifies hazards associated with selling a home, describes them in some detail, and provides guidance to avoid them or deal with them.

How to Sell Your Home Fast, for the Highest Price, in Any Market by Terry Eilers (New York: Hyperion, 1997). Takes the reader through every step of the sale process, from finding a qualified agent and establishing a list price, to marketing and advertising the house and managing details of the closing.

How to Sell Your Home without a Broker, 3rd ed. by Bill Carey, Chantal Howell Carey, and Suzanne Kiffmann (Hoboken, NJ: John Wiley & Sons, 2000). Explains how to prepare your property for sale and how to find buyers so that you can avoid paying the real estate broker's commission.

Seller Beware: Insider Secrets You Need to Know About Selling Your House —From Listing through Closing the Deal by Robert Irwin (Chicago IL: Dearborn Financial Publishing, 1998). Tells readers how to navigate safely around the problems that can arise from an undisclosed defect in a home. Explains what defects to disclose (all), when to disclose them (up front), what to fix, and what to leave.

Sell It Yourself by Ralph Roberts (Holbrook, MA: Adams Media Corp., 1999). How to sell your home without a broker.

Tips and Traps When Selling a Home, 3rd ed., by Robert Irwin (New York: McGraw-Hill, 2003). Offers strategies for getting the highest price possible for your home. Gives advice on sprucing up your property, using a real estate broker, and negotiating with buyers.

▶ Web sites with additional information on specific topics

For Chapter 1

To locate a qualified estate planning attorney:

- ▶ American College of Trust and Estate Counsel (ACTEC) at http://www.actec.org or write to the ACTEC, 3415 South Sepulveda Boulevard, Suite 330, Los Angeles, CA 90034.

For Chapter 3

- ▶ Social Security Administration (800-772-1213; http://www.ssa.gov).

  For calculating retirement savings:

- ▶ One simple program, called the *Retirement Planning Analyzer,* is available for $20 from T. Rowe Price Associates (100 E. Pratt St., Baltimore, MD 21202; 800-541-1472; http://www.troweprice.com). Other personal finance programs such as *Quicken* and *Microsoft Money* also have retirement planning sections.

- ▶ Disclosure requirements for state-registered financial advisors vary, so check with your state's securities department to find out what's required in your state. The North American Securities Administrators Association (NASAA) can provide you with more information about these requirements at 888-846-2722.

You can also contact the Federal Trade Commission (6th St. and Pennsylvania Ave., N.W., Washington, DC 20580; 202-326-2222; 877-FTC-HELP; http://www.ftc.gov). It offers many helpful brochures, including:

▶ Facts about Financial Planners
▶ How to Talk To and Select Lawyers, Financial Planners, Tax Preparers and Real Estate Brokers.

It also lists FTC publications, Consumer Alerts, Education Campaigns, and the Consumer's Action Handbook, and allows you to lodge fraud complaints against financial planners.

In addition, the following Web sites are for companies that rate brokerage firms:

▶ American Association of Individual Investors; http://www.aaii.com
▶ Gomez, Inc.; http://www.gomez.com
▶ JD Power and Associates; http://www.jdpower.com
▶ Kiplinger's Personal Finance; http://www.kiplinger.com
▶ Smart Money; http://www.smartmoney.com
▶ Money; http://www.pathfinder.com
▶ Keynote Systems; http://www.keynote.com
▶ Forrester Power Rankings; http://www.forrester.com
▶ Barron's; http://www.wsj.com
▶ CNNfn; http://www.cnnfn.com
▶ Worth Magazine; http://www.worth.com

Finally, you can contact your state's attorney general for background information on financial planners; check the blue pages in your telephone directory.

To find fee-only financial planners:

▶ National Association of Personal Financial Advisors (NAPFA) in Buffalo Grove, Illinois (888-FEE-ONLY), the largest association of fee-only planners, will supply a list of fee-only planners.
▶ Financial Planning Association Adviser Referral Program (800-322-4237 or http://www.fpanet.org) will send brochures explaining the financial planning process and how to select a financial advisor, an interview sheet to guide you through the selection process, and detailed background information on three advisors who match the criteria you specify.

► The Garrett Planning Network, Inc. (866-260-8400; http://www.garrett planningnetwork.com) is an international network of independent financial advisors and planners offering hourly as-needed financial planning and advice to anyone regardless of income.

For Chapter 4

To compare insurance companies:

► *Annuity Shopper,* 8 Talmadge Dr., Monroe TWP, NJ 08831. 800-872-6684; 908-521-5110.
► For an exhaustive analysis of how much insurance you need, run through the exercises available on software like Microsoft Money or Quicken or contact an independent insurance advisor through the Life Insurance Advisers Association (800-521-4578), who will counsel you about your insurance needs; they sell no policies.

For information on life insurance payments from government programs:

► Call the Social Security Administration, the Department of Veterans Affairs (VA), or your employee benefits office.

For price quotes on term life insurance: you can obtain price quotes on term coverage through any insurance agent, many direct mail insurers, banks, or quote services such as:

► AccuQuote
► BestQuote
► Choice Quote
► INSurance INFOrmation
► Insurance Quote
► QuickQuote
► QuoteSmith
► Selectquote
► TermQuote

For information on how to find annuity-type life insurance and to find annuities, consult a recent issue of the following publications:

► *Variable Annuity Research & Data Service Large Report* (P.O. Box 1927, Roswell, GA 30077-1927. 770-998-5186);

▶ *Comparative Annuity Reports* (P.O. Box 1268, Fair Oaks, CA 95628. 916-487-7863); or

▶ *Annuity Shopper* (8 Talmadge Dr., Monroe TWP, NJ 08831. 800-872-6684; 908-521-5110).

For help evaluating managed care health insurance plans:

▶ National Committee for Quality Assurance (2000 L St., N.W., Suite 500, Washington, DC 20036. 202-955-3500; 800-839-6787. http://www.ncqa. org), a private, not-for-profit organization dedicated to assessing and reporting on the quality of managed care plans.

▶ To find out whether a managed care program is accredited by NCQA, call their Accreditation Status Line at 202-955-5697, or download their Accreditation Status List from their Web site. NCQA also provides two-page Accreditation Summary Reports giving you more detail on the performance of a particular plan.

For more health insurance information:

▶ Contact a health insurance agent or broker to help you find the policy that best suits your needs. Many agents have access to computerized services that help them locate the policies offering the most coverage for the least price. The three largest insurance services are Quotesmith (800-556-9393); Dinan (800-346-2610); and Group Benefit Shoppers (800-231-8495). If the agent you choose does not have access to these services, call one of these services and ask for an agent near you who does subscribe.

For more details on the expenses Medicare covers, as well as the cost of deductibles, co-payments, and premiums:

▶ Call the Social Security Administration's Medicare hotline at 800-772-1213, or obtain a copy of the *Medicare Handbook* from any Social Security office.

For a more detailed look at the best long-term health care solutions:

▶ *Long-Term Care: A Dollars and Sense Guide,* published by the United Seniors Health Cooperative (1331 H St., N.W., Suite 500, Washington, DC 20005. 202-393-6222; http://www.ushc-online.org). The publication discusses the many aspects of long-term care, including continuing care communities, nursing homes, and veterans' options.

▶ Another helpful unbiased source for the best long-term care policies is Long Term Care Quote (600 W. Ray Rd., Suite D4, Chandler, AZ 85224. 800-587-3279; http://www.ltcq.com).

For more details on Social Security disability insurance:

▶ Call the Social Security Administration (800-772-1213; http://www.ssa.gov), request the brochure, "When You Get Social Security Disability Benefits...What You Need to Know."

For more information on buying long-term care insurance, see:

▶ The National Association of Insurance Commissioners publishes "Shopper's Guide to Long-Term Care Insurance" (http://www.naic.org/insprod/store_home.htm).

Best Web sites for insurance information

Here are some of the best insurance information sites to find solid educational content, policy quotes, or links to quote services. Doing your homework ahead of time can save you money on premiums—and headaches down the road.

▶ About Disability Insurance (http://www.about-disability-insurance.com). Provides descriptions of the major features of a disability insurance policy and links to other Web sites.

▶ E.F. Moody (http://www.efmoody.com). Life and disability insurance analyst. Features financial information as well as an overview of insurance.

▶ Federal Emergency Management Agency flood insurance information (http://www.fema.gov/nfip/whonfip.shtm). The only option for flood coverage, this site provides information about the coverage and how to get it.

▶ Health Insurance Information (http://www.healthinsuranceinfo.net). A resource to maintain health insurance once COBRA coverage expires; see the Consumer Guides for Getting and Keeping Insurance for each state.

▶ Insurance Information Institute (http://www.iii.org). Provides the public with information about insurance and the insurance industry.

- ▶ Insure Kids Now (http://www.insurekidsnow.gov). Provides information on free or low-cost health insurance to children of lower-income families who do not have health insurance.
- ▶ Medicare (http://cms.hhs.gov/medicaid). Medigap plan comparisons, Medicare health plans comparison, consumer publications; also, includes directories of potential sources of additional assistance with care expenses.
- ▶ National Association of Insurance Commissioners (http://www.naic.org). Consumer interest site featuring a directory of state insurance regulators and catalog of educational publications.

Insurance Rating Agencies and Helpful Sites

- ▶ A.M. Best Company (http://www.ambest.com)
- ▶ Anthony Steuer Insurance Services (http://www.tonysteuer.com/res_RatingServices.html)
- ▶ Coalition against Insurance Fraud—Scam Alerts and Insurance Fraud Hall of Shame (http://www.insurancefraud.org)
- ▶ Fitch Ratings, Ltd. (http://www.fitchratings.com)
- ▶ Moody's Investor Services (http://www.moodys.com)
- ▶ Standard and Poor's Corporation (http://www.standardandpoors.com)
- ▶ Weiss Research (http://www.weissratings.com)

Shopping Sites to Compare and Obtain Insurance Quotes

- ▶ http://www.insweb.com
- ▶ http://www.insure.com
- ▶ http://www.ehealthinsurance.com
- ▶ http://moneycentral.msn.com/insure/welcome.asp

For Chapter 5

To track the highest yields on CDs:

- ▶ Check out *The Wall Street Journal* and *USA Today,* as well as the "Monitor" section of *Money* magazine. You also can look up the highest yields on Web sites such as http://www.bankrate.com or http://www.imoneynet.com.
- ▶ Or, you can subscribe to the newsletter *100 Highest Yields* (P.O. Box 088888, North Palm Beach, FL 33408. 800-327-7717), which surveys banks

every week to uncover those with the top yields for 6-month, 1-year, 2½-year, and 5-year certificates.

For more information on how savings bonds work:

▶ Contact any Federal Reserve Bank, or write the Savings Bond Office at the U.S. Treasury, 999 E St., N.W., Washington, DC 20239. You can call that office at 202-447-1775 or find the latest savings bond rates at 800-872-6637.

▶ Other good sources of information are the Treasury's Web site at http://www.savingsbonds.gov and the Savings Bond Informer (P.O. Box 09249, Detroit, MI 48209; 313-843-1910. 800-927-1901).

For information on buying shares in a zero-coupon bond *mutual fund*:

▶ The largest fund company offering zero-coupon funds is American Century Investments (P.O. Box 419200, Kansas City, MO 64141. 800-345-2021. http://www.americancentury.com), which offers the no-load Benham Target Maturities Trusts that are set to mature every five years. You pay annual expenses of .62 percent of your assets.

For more information on convertible bonds:

▶ Many brokerage firms publish research reports on widely traded issues. The best newsletter that tracks the field is the *Value Line Convertibles* (220 E. 42nd St., New York, NY 10017. 800-535-8760).

For more information on UITs:

▶ You can request a free guide to UITs called "An Overture to Our Investment Strategy," by calling 877-DEFINED, 877-333-4633, ext. 3199. This guide is published by Merrill Lynch, Pierce, Fenner & Smith Inc.

For information on investing clubs:

▶ The easiest way to get your club started is to send away for the step-by-step manual published by the NAIC (P.O. Box 220, Royal Oak, MI 48068. 248-583-6242; 877-275-6242. http://www.better-investing.org). The guide will tell you how to get a federal tax identification number, open a brokerage account, and set up a recordkeeping system so the club's treasurer can track deposits and withdrawals.

For more detailed information on how reverse mortgages work and which institutions currently grant them:

▶ National Center for Home Equity Conversion (360 N. Robert, Suite 403, St. Paul, MN 55101. 651-222-6775. http://www.reverse.org). Publisher of *Retirement Income on the House: Cashing In on Your Home with a "Reverse" Mortgage,* which describes how reverse mortgages work and includes a "Reverse Mortgage Locator," which lists all reverse mortgage lenders in the country.

Index

Page numbers shown in *italic* indicate references to a Roadmap, Tollbooth, or What to Pack feature.